THE CITY.

PAVED WITH GOLD

A Scrapbook of London Life

ESMOR JONES

Blackie

Blackie & Son Limited
Bishopbriggs, Glasgow G64 2NZ
5 Fitzhardinge Street, London W1H 0DL

Educational Edition ISBN 0 216 89930 3
General Edition ISBN 0 216 89891 9

Printed in Great Britain by
Robert MacLehose & Company Limited, Glasgow

Foreword

London can look very permanent to the casual visitor—a city of great streets and historic buildings. There was the American I met at the top of the Hilton who gazed vaguely down at roads, houses and parks and murmured "How quaint!" He saw nothing of the new skyscrapers and office blocks. Perhaps they were too familiar to be noticed.

But London is changing. It has been changing rapidly throughout the last two hundred years. For the metropolis is a shifting amalgam of homes and places of work. People and trade, as always, live side by side and intermingle. London is also a city where people do not live but only work. So, in another sense, it is a communications network.

It has always been an area of great contrasts, especially in ways of life. Too often the splendid facades have masked poverty. London is the capital city, the centre of power. It is also the "home" of the rootless and of those with no power at all.

The material in this book is almost wholly contemporary. Through it we can look at the lives of the people of London and at how they have felt about their city. Throughout, the face of London is altering but it is worth looking for the similarities in life in other generations. We start with the comparatively static London of the eighteenth century and then see what new kind of life was born from the revolution in industry and transport. The London of the nineteenth century has gone now. The internal combustion engine and the bombs have violently changed the appearance of much of the city.

But the past is still there to see—layer upon layer of it. And the Londoner of the 1970s is clearly a true descendant of his rougher eighteenth century forbears.

ESMOR JONES

Acknowledgments

For permission to reproduce copyright material in this anthology, the compiler and publisher would like to thank the following:
The Science Museum, London for the frontispiece and the photographs on pages 25, 26.
The Radio Times Hulton Picture Library for the photographs on pages 2, 4, 6, 12, 16, 18, 22, 24, 30, 33, 34, 37, 42, 46, 56, 59, 62, 64, 72, 75, 79.
The Mansell Collection for the photographs on pages 9, 53.
The Salvation Army Information Service for the photograph on page 49.
Maurice Rickards Esq. for the print of the postcard 'Skegness is *so* bracing' on page 66.
Longman Group Limited for the extract from *English Social History* by G. M. Trevelyan.
Leslie Paul for the extract from *The Boy Down Kitchener Street* by Leslie Paul; also for the extracts from *The Living Hedge* by Leslie Paul.
Oxford University Press for the extracts from *A London Child of the Seventies* by M. Vivian Hughes.
The Architectural Press Limited for the extract from "Seventy Years Back" by H. B. Cresswell in *The Architectural Review* (December 1958).
Barrie & Jenkins Limited for the poem "Days Drawing In" by E. J. Scovell from *The First Year*.
Cassell & Company Limited for the extract from *The Second World War: Volume II* by Winston S. Churchill.
The Hogarth Press for the extract from "The Wall" from *The Stories of William Sansom* © William Sansom 1963.
Routledge & Keegan Paul Limited for the extract from *Family and Kinship in East London* by M. Young & P. Willmott; for the extracts from *Adolescent Boys in East London* by P. Willmott; for the extract from *Family and Class in a London Suburb* by P. Willmott & M. Young.
William Kimber & Co. Limited for the extract from *London Morning* by Valerie Avery.
Weidenfeld & Nicolson for the extract from *The World Cities* by Peter Hall.
The English Association for the poem "Arrival" by Ee Tiang Hong and the poem "The Lament of the Banana Man" by Evan Jones from *Commonwealth Poems of Today*.
MacGibbon & Kee for the extracts from *Absolute Beginners* by Colin MacInnes.
Every effort has been made to trace copyright holders, but any inadvertent omissions will be rectified.

Contents

Prologue

I have often amused myself with thinking how different a place London is to different people. They, whose narrow minds are contracted to the consideration of some one particular pursuit, view it only through that medium . . . But the intellectual man is struck with it, as comprehending the whole of human life in all its variety, the contemplation of which is inexhaustible.

James Boswell (1791) from *Boswell's Life of Johnson*

For many years now variety has gone from the City. There the teeming day-time population contrasts with a five-thousand night population. What has happened in the City is happening to the West End. The claim of many who have offices in the West End is that for their clients and customers they have the amenities of the hotels, the clubs, the restaurants, and for their staff the shops and the parks. If the process goes on, these very advantages will be gobbled up and the West End will become one dreary sea of office blocks.

from Journal of the Town Planning Institute (January 1959)

Fleet Street—a London thoroughfare

I talked of the cheerfulness of Fleet Street, owing to the constant quick succession of people which we perceive passing through it. JOHNSON. "Why, Sir, Fleet Street has a very animated appearance; but I think the full tide of human existence is at Charing-cross."

I suggested a doubt, that if I were to reside in London, the exquisite zest with which I relished it on occasional visits might go off. JOHNSON. "Why, Sir, you find no man, at all intellectual, who is willing to leave London. No, Sir, when a man is tired of London, he is tired of life; for there is in London all that life can afford."

We talked of living in the country. JOHNSON. "No wise man will go to live in the country, unless he has something to do which can be better done in the country. For instance; if he is to shut himself up for a year to study a science, it is better to look out to the fields, than to an opposite wall. Then, if a man walks out in the country, there is nobody to keep him from walking in again; but if a man walks out in London, he is not sure when he shall walk in again. A great city is, to be sure, the school for studying life; and 'The proper study of mankind is man', as Pope observes."

from *Boswell's Life of Johnson*

The Lure of London

Young men and women in the country fix their eye on London as the last stage of their hope; they enter into service in the country for little else but to raise money enough to go to London, which was no such easy matter when a stage coach was four or five days creeping an hundred miles; and the fare and the expenses ran high. But now! a country fellow one hundred miles from London jumps onto a coach-box in the morning, and for eight or ten shillings gets to town by night, which makes a material difference; besides rendering the going up and down so easy that the numbers who have seen London are increased tenfold and of course ten times the boasts are sounded in the ears of country fools, to induce them to quit their healthy clean fields for a region of dirt, stink and noise. And the number of young women that fly thither is almost incredible.

Arthur Young

The Idle 'Prentice betrayed by a prostitute

London Awakes

Now hardly here and there an Hackney-Coach
Appearing show'd the Ruddy Morn's approach.
Now Betty from her Master's Bed had flown,
And softly stole to discompose her own.
The slipshod 'Prentice from his Master's Door,
Had par'd the street, and sprinkled round the Floor.
Now Moll had whirl'd her mop with dextrous airs,
Prepar'd to scrub the Entry and the Stairs.
The Youth with broomy stumps began to trace
The Kennel Edge, where wheels had worn the place.
The Smallcoal-Man was heard with cadence deep,
Till drown'd in shriller notes of Chimney-sweep.
Duns at his Lordship's Gate began to meet;
And Brickdust Moll had scream'd through half a street.
The Turn-key now his Flock returning sees,
Duly let out a' nights to steal for fees.
The watchful Bailiffs take their silent stands;
And Schoolboys lag with satchels in their hands.

from "Description of a Morning" by Jonathan Swift

Heavy rain in old London revealed the insanitary state of the city and
its inadequate drains (or kennels):

Now from all parts the swelling Kennels flow,
And bear their trophies with them as they go:
Filth of all hues and odours seem to tell
What street they sail'd from, by their sight or smell.
They, as each torrent drives, with rapid force
From Smithfield or St Pulchre's shape their course,
And in huge confluent join at Snow-Hill Ridge,
Fall from the Conduit prone to Holborn-Bridge.
Sweepings from Butchers' Stalls, dung, guts, and blood,
Drown'd puppies, stinking sprats, all drench'd in mud,
Dead cats and turnip-tops come tumbling down the flood.

from "Description of a Shower" by Jonathan Swift

Frost Fair on the Thames, 1683

1st January. The weather continuing intolerably severe, streets of booths were set upon the Thames; the air was so very cold and thick, as of many years there had not been the like. The smallpox was very mortal.

2nd I dined at Sir Stephen Fox's: after dinner came a fellow who eat live charcoal, glowingly ignited, quenching them in his mouth, and then champing and swallowing them down. There was a dog also which seemed to do many rational actions.

6th The river quite frozen.

9th I went across the Thames on the ice, now become so thick as to bear not only streets of booths, in which they roasted meat, and had divers shops of wares, quite across as in a town, but coaches, carts, and horses passed over. So I went from Westminster-stairs to Lambeth, and dined with the Archbishop: where I met my Lord Bruce, Sir George Wheeler, Colonel Cooke, and several divines. After dinner and discourse with his Grace till evening prayers, Sir

George Wheeler and I walked over the ice from Lambeth-stairs to the Horse-ferry.

16*th* The Thames was filled with people and tents, selling all sorts of wares as in the City.

24*th* The frost continuing more and more severe, the Thames before London was still planted with booths in formal streets, all sorts of trades and shops furnished, and full of commodities, even to a printing-press, where the people and ladies took a fancy to have their names printed, and the day and the year set down when printed on the Thames: this humour took so universally, that it was estimated the printer gained £5 a day, for printing a line only, at sixpence a name, besides what he got by ballads, &c. Coaches plied from Westminster to the Temple, and from several other stairs to and fro, as in the streets, sleds, sliding with skates, a bull-baiting, horse and coach-races, puppet-plays, and interludes, cooks, and tippling, so that it seemed to be a bacchanalian triumph, or carnival on the water, whilst it was a severe judgment on the land, the trees not only splitting as if lightning-struck, but men and cattle perishing in divers places, and the very seas so locked up with ice, that no vessels could stir out or come in. The fowls, fish, and birds, and all our exotic plants and greens, universally perishing. Many parks of deer were destroyed, and all sorts of fuel so dear, that there were great contributions to preserve the poor alive. Nor was this severe weather much less intense in most parts of Europe, even as far as Spain and the most southern tracts. London, by reason of the excessive coldness of the air hindering the ascent of the smoke, was so filled with the fuliginous steam of the sea-coal, that hardly could one see across the streets, and this filling the lungs with its gross particles, exceedingly obstructed the breast, so as one could scarcely breathe. Here was no water to be had from the pipes and engines, nor could the brewers and divers other tradesmen work, and every moment was full of disastrous accidents.

from John Evelyn's Diary for 1683

Hell is a city much like London —
  A populous and a smoky city;
There are all sorts of people undone;
And there is little or no fun done;
  Small justice shown, and still less pity.

from "Peter Bell the Third" by Percy Bysshe Shelley

London is a Fine Town

O London is a dainty place,
  A great and gallant city!
For all the Streets are pav'd with gold,
  And all the folks are witty.
And there's your lords and ladies fine,
  That ride in coach and six;
That nothing drink but claret wine,
  And talk of politicks.

And there's your beaux with powder'd clothes,
  Bedaub'd from head to chin;
Their pocket-holes adorned with gold,
  But not one sous within.
And there the English actor goes
  With many a hungry belly;
While heaps of gold are forc'd, God wot,
  On Signor Farinelli.

And there's your dames with dainty frames,
  With skins as white as milk;
Dressed every day in garments gay,
  Of satin and of silk.
And if your mind be so inclined
  To offer them your arm,
Pull out a handsome purse of gold,
  They can't resist the charm.

Anon.

The Great Fire of London, 1666

Old London has two great streets that run parallel to the Thames; the Strand, which, being joined to Fleet Street and Cheapside, extends the whole length of the town; and Holborn, which is cut in a disagreeable manner by the prison of Newgate. These two streets are of a good breadth, but not exactly regular. St Paul's is the object which should naturally terminate the view in the Strand, but after walking a long time in this street, we do not discover that fine cathedral till we come close to the building.

We should read the inscription on the monument erected by Charles the Second a little above London Bridge, to convince ourselves that in the reign of this prince a great part of Old London was rebuilt upon a new plan. Houses scattered about at random could not form streets more narrow or irregular. If the inhabitants could think they had any reason to congratulate themselves upon the change, it must be from a comparison of the present with the primitive state of those quarters, before they were consumed by fire, and because when they had gained a little ground by injuring property, which is held very sacred in England, they thought they had done great matters. That part of London must then have been in a more wretched condition than the quarter of Paris called the City. With what rapidity must the fire have spread amongst a confused heap of buildings all of which were of wood! for it was not till the reign of King James the First that they began to build with brick.

In this quarter of London rebuilt after the Great Fire, the streets which were paved in such a manner that it was scarce possible to find a place to set one's foot, and absolutely impossible to ride in a coach, are eternally covered with dirt.

The longest and finest streets, such as the Strand, Cheapside, Holborn, etc., would be unpassable, if there were not, for the conveniency of those who are on foot, paths on each side of the way four or five feet broad; and, to make a communication between these across the street, little causeways raised above the level of it, and made of the broadest stones picked out with the utmost care for this purpose. It is easy to see what great disadvantages must result from these numerous causeways to carriages.

In the most beautiful part of the Strand and near St Clement's Church, I have, during my whole stay in London, seen the middle of the street constantly foul with a dirty puddle to the height of three or four inches; a puddle where splashings cover those who walk on foot, fill coaches when their windows happen not to be up, and bedaub all the lower parts of such houses as are exposed to it. In consequence of this, the prentices are frequently employed in washing the fronts of their houses, in order to take off the daubing of dirt which they had contracted overnight.

The English are not afraid of this dirt, being defended from it by their wigs of a brownish curling hair, their black stockings, and their blue surtouts which are made in the form of a nightgown.

To enable the reader to judge how frequently this daubing must happen, it will be sufficient to inform him that the pavement of London is formed on stones just as when taken out of the quarry. These stones, which are almost entirely round, have neither tail, foot, nor any part so formed as to stand upon; they roll about and hit one another incessantly upon a bottom, which is nothing else but a heap of old dirt. The whole art of the paviour consists in placing these stones as near each other as possible; yet, bad as it is, this pavement is exceeding dear, there being no materials for it in the neighbourhood of London, but sand, gravel, and chalk. With regard to the free-stone pavement, the materials of it are brought at a great expense from the extremities of the kingdom, and it is one of the dearest commodities in London. If we may believe a story told by the people of London, Lewis the Fourteenth offered to supply Charles the Second with free-stone to pave his capital, upon condition that the English monarch should furnish him with that fine gravel with which the English strew the walks in their gardens and which when well rolled assumes the smoothness of a bowling green.

Means however have been found to pave with free-stone the the great street called Parliament Street, which reaches from Westminster Abbey to Charing Cross. The fine street called Pall-Mall is already paved in part with this stone, and they have also begun to new pave the Strand. The two first of these streets were dry in May, all the rest of the town being still covered with heaps of dirt; it was even customary to water them as well as the bridges and the high roads in the neighbourhood of London: this has been a practice in England time out of mind.

Those that walk may preserve themselves from the perplexity and dirt of the most frequented streets, by turning into courts between the Strand and Holborn, which are joined together by passages or alleys that are shown to a stranger by the crowds continually passing to and fro.

The finest shops are scattered up and down in these courts and passages. The grand company which they draw together, the elegant arrangement and parade made by the shops, whether in stuffs exposed to sale, fine furniture, and things of taste, or the girls belonging to them, would be motives sufficient to determine those that walk, to make that their way in preference to any other, even if they had not neatness and security to recommend them.

Except in the two or three streets which have very lately been well paved, the best hung and the richest coaches are in point of ease as bad as carts; whether this be owing to the tossing occasioned at every step by the inequality and instability of the pavement, or to the continual danger of being splashed if all the windows are not kept constantly up.

from A Tour to England by Pierre Jean Grosley

Carriages in Hyde Park

The hackney coaches in London are a great convenience. About one thousand of these vehicles are to be found day and night in the public places and principal streets of the city and town. Most of them, to tell the truth, are ugly and dirty. The driver is perched high up on a wooden seat, as elevated as the imperial of a coach. The body of the carriage is very badly balanced, so that when inside you are most cruelly shaken, the pavement being very uneven, and most of the horses excellent and fast trotters. A drive costs one shilling, provided you do not go further than a certain distance; other drives will cost two or sometimes three shillings, according to distance. The drivers often ask more than is their due, and this is the case especially when they have to do with foreigners. To avoid being cheated, you must take the number of the coach marked on the door, and offer the driver a handful of coins, telling him to take his fare out of it. In this fashion of dealing he will not take more than his due, for should he do so you have the right to go and complain at the coach office, and the driver will be punished by being made to pay a fine, half of which would go to the plaintiff, and the other half to the officers of the office.

Besides these conveyances there are a great number of chariots and coaches belonging to noblemen and to gentlemen. Some are magnificent, and most are drawn by fine and excellent horses. The chariots belonging to noblemen are recognizable by the small gilt coronets placed at each of the four corners of the imperial; those belonging to dukes have ducal coronets, and so on. These fine chariots behind which stand two or three footmen attired in rich liveries, are certainly a great ornament to a town, and a convenience to rich people, but they are a great hindrance to those who are not wealthy and go on foot, for the streets being generally very muddy, the passers-by get terribly bespattered and dirty. Pedestrians, it is true, would be far worse off were there not on either side of the street a sort of elevated footpath for their convenience.

Near the palace and in its vicinity there are more than three hundred sedan chairs for hire; like the cabs, they are found in the principal streets and thoroughfares. Chairs are very convenient and pleasant for use, the bearers going so fast that you have some difficulty in keeping up with them on foot. I do not believe that in the whole of Europe better or more dexterous bearers are to be found; all foreigners are surprised at their strength and skill. Like coaches, sedan chairs are most convenient for the wealthy, but often very embarrassing for those of another class, for these chairs are allowed to be carried on the foot-paths, and when a person does not take heed, or a stranger does not understand the "Have care", or "By your leave, sir," of the bearers, and does not make room to let them pass, he will run a great risk of being knocked down, for the bearers go very fast and cannot turn aside with their burden.

I went through this experience on first coming to London. Not understanding the "By your leave" addressed to me, I did not draw aside, and repented quickly, for I received a tremendous push which hurled me four feet further on, and I should undoubtedly have fallen on my back had it not been for the wall of a house which broke my fall, but much to the injury of my arm. To my cost I thus learnt what the cry of the bearer means. Sedan chairs are also numbered and there is an office where you can go and make your complaint if cheated by your bearers.

from *A Foreign View of England in the Reigns of George I and George II from letters of César de Saussure to his Family*

Lydia Melford, a country girl, writes to her friend:

About five days ago we arrived in London, after an easy journey from Bath; during which, however, we were overturned, and met some other little incidents, which, had like to have occasioned a misunderstanding betwixt my uncle and aunt; but now, thank God, they are happily reconciled: we live in harmony together and every day make parties to see the wonders of this vast metropolis, which, however, I cannot pretend to describe; for I have not as yet seen one hundredth part of its curiosities, and I am quite in a maze of admiration.

The cities of London and Westminster are spread out into an incredible extent. The streets, squares, rows, lanes, and alleys, are innumerable. Palaces, public buildings, and churches rise in every quarter; and, among these last, St Paul's appears with the most astonishing pre-eminence. They say it is not so large as St Peter's at Rome; but, for my own part, I can have no idea of any earthly temple more grand and magnificent.

But even these superb objects are not so striking as the crowds of people that swarm in the streets. I at first imagined that some great assembly was just dismissed, and wanted to stand aside till the multitude should pass; but this human tide continues to flow, without interruption or abatement, from morn till night. Then there is such an infinity of gay equipages, coaches, chariots, chaises, and other carriages, continually rolling and shifting before your eyes, that one's head grows giddy looking at them; and the imagination is quite confounded with splendour and variety. Nor is the prospect by water less grand and astonishing than that by land: you see three stupendous bridges, joining the opposite banks of a broad, deep, and rapid river; so vast, so stately, so elegant, that they seem to be the work of the giants; betwixt them, the whole surface of the Thames is covered with small vessels, barges, boats, and wherries, passing to and fro; and below the three bridges, such a prodigious forest of masts, for miles together, that you would think all the ships in the universe were here assembled. All that you read of wealth and grandeur in the *Arabian Nights Entertainment*, and the *Persian Tales*, concerning Bagdad, Diarbekir, Damascus, Ispahan, and Samarkand, is here realized.

Ranelagh looks like the enchanted palace of a genie, adorned with the most exquisite performances of painting, carving, and gilding, enlightened with a thousand golden lamps, that emulate the noon-day sun; crowded with the great, the rich, the gay, the happy, and the fair; glittering with cloth of gold and silver, lace, embroidery, and precious stones. While these exulting sons and daughters of felicity tread this round of pleasure, or regale in different parties, and separate lodges, with fine imperial tea and other delicious refreshments, their ears are entertained with the most ravishing delights of music, both instrumental and vocal. There I heard the famous Tenducci, a thing from Italy—It looks for all the world like a man, though they say it is not. The voice, to be sure, is neither man's nor woman's; but it is more melodious than either; and it warbled so divinely, that, while I listened, I really thought myself in paradise.

At nine o'clock, in a charming moonlight evening, we embarked at Ranelagh for Vauxhall . . . which I no sooner entered, than I was dazzled and confounded with the variety of beauties that rushed all at once upon my eye. Image to yourself, my dear Letty, a spacious garden, part laid out in delightful walks, bounded with high hedges and trees, and paved with gravel; part exhibiting a wonderful assemblage of the most picturesque and striking objects, pavilions, lodges, groves, grottoes, lawns, temples, and cascades; porticoes, colonnades, and rotundas; adorned with pillars, statues, and paint-ing: the whole illuminated with an infinite number of lamps, disposed in different figures of suns, stars, and constellations; the place crowded with the gayest company, ranging through those blissful shades, or supping in different lodges on cold collations, enlivened with mirth, freedom, and good humour, and animated by an excellent band of music.

from Humphrey Clinker by Tobias Smollett

Views in Vauxhall Gardens

1. Fountain at back of orchestra; 2. Ruins at end of walk; 3. The orchestra;
4. Neptune's fountain; 5. Old entrance to Vauxhall Gardens; 6. Back of
orchestra.

The Pleasures of Old London

A further description of Vauxhall:

The Grove was the square enclosed by the Grand and South Walks, and by the Cross Walk and the western wall of the gardens, and it was the centre of the buildings of Vauxhall which came to be as famous as its groves and arbours. Round and about the temples, the pavilions, the rotundas, the great rooms, the music rooms, the picture rooms, the covered colonnades for wet weather, above all the famous supper boxes built in straight rows or curving sweeps. In those famous supper boxes, where generations of Londoners ate the noted Vauxhall chicken and ham, were the paintings which gave a quaint interest to each, every picture displayed by its own little oil lamp. There were the "Four Times of a Day", copied by permission from Mr Hogarth's noted compositions of the same title, and the varied productions of Mr Francis Hayman and other artists; scenes from Shakespeare and from popular comedies; representations of the favourite sports of the people—the Play of See-saw, the Play of Cricket, Leap-Frog, Sliding on the Ice, milkmaids dancing round the Maypole, Phyllis and Corydon, pipe and tabor, sheep and shepherds and shepherdesses and what not. Mr Hogarth himself painted a picture for one of the larger saloons, of Henry the Eighth and Anne Boleyn; and in his blunt way, it is said, pointed to a famous scandal of the day by painting Henry with the face of Frederick, Prince of Wales, and Lady Archibald Hamilton as Anne Boleyn. Above all, Mr Tyers lighted up the darkness of his groves "with above a thousand lamps so disposed that they all took fire together, with such a sudden blaze as was perfectly surprising".

It was the same lighting of the groves which formed one of the chief attractions of Vauxhall and captivated all beholders for half a century. There is a continual rhapsody on the lamps at Vauxhall by generations of writers, and a blaze of artificial light seen through a foreground of overhanging trees at Vauxhall provided a subject for a succession of artists, who produced those delightful vignettes on copper for its programmes and song sheets where the beauties of the place are best preserved. The illuminations of Vauxhall were undoubtedly arranged with much taste, and the sudden lighting of the lamps, with a simultaneous crash of music from the orchestra, had a considerable effect. Moreover, the illuminations of Vauxhall gained greatly by contrast with the aspect of the town of that day. Long after the general use of gas, London after nightfall was a dull and gloomy place. The streets were generally narrow and ill lighted, and quite without the blaze of light to which we are accustomed from the modern shop window. Even at the theatres, the stage effects, with which this century is familiar, were unknown, and Vauxhall was really the only place where the citizens could see anything of the beauty of artificial light intelligently employed. Modern caterers are fully aware of the value of a judicious investment in gas and white paint, and there is little wonder at the success of the efforts of Mr Tyers and his successors to produce "a rich blaze of radiance" by their coloured lamps and chandeliers and illuminated stars and revolving mirrors in an age when the ordinary surroundings of the Londoner gave them so much help by their contrast.

from *Amusements of Old London* by W. J. Boulton

★   ★   ★   ★   ★

A Gambling House

Gambling, by Regency times, had become a curse. William Crockford fleeced the nobility and set the example for the rest of London society:

The immediate result of the organization's operations in London was the establishment of cheap gaming-houses all over the town. Hazard revived, or rather descended from Brooks's and the Cocoa Tree to shady houses in Soho, Covent Garden, and the City, and people of humble condition were taught the joys and the dangers of roulette, *rouge et noir*, and macao for small stakes. Morley's was a noted cheap hazard-house in the City, Miller's a famous hell of the low type in Leicester Street, where loaded dice were habitually used, and drunken clerks relieved of their employers' money a hundred pounds at a time. John Taylor, of the Bedford Arms, Covent Garden, stood a seige of some hours against the sheriff's officers, having thoughtfully provided his passages with doors of wrought-iron. No. 19 Great Suffolk Street had a subterranean passage into an empty house in Whitcombe Street, through which proprietors and customers escaped when the place was raided. At No. 3 Leicester Square there was an exit over the roofs, but one gentleman mistaking it was smoked out of the chimney by the officers. Every other house in the piazza of Covent Garden seems to have been raided, but the profits were so great that the fines were easily paid, and if a man here or there was imprisoned, his partners carried on the business at another place during his absence, and he came out to share the profits which had accumulated while he was doing his term. "I can easily pay £500," said Mr Miller of Leicester Square after a second raid; he paid that sum, did his two years, and opened again round the corner.

The mischief these places did is almost incalculable; bankruptcies, embezzlements, duels, and suicides resulting from gaming were of weekly occurrence, and it would seem that half the tradesmen and clerks of London were before the magistrates or the coroners of the last years of the last century and the first quarter of this. Men sat at these houses for a week at a time, and ended by losing the clothes from their back and being turned out in their stockings and shirt, and perhaps the climax was reached when two men were interrupted in preparations for an execution on a lamp-post in the north of London, the one having lost his life to the other for the sake of the clothes to be gathered from the corpse.

★　★　★　★　★

There were rougher amusements. Finally, the great tradition of St Bartholomew's Fair came to an end in disorder. So did Southwark Fair.

In addition to all other attractions of the fair was that chance of turbulence, disorder, and horseplay always dear to a crowd of Englishmen. Lady Holland's Mob was an evergreen which flourished through season after season, and was always ready at a moment's notice to join issue with the powers represented by the constables of the corporation. The periodical suppression of the booths in the early part of the century was a frequent opportunity for their exertions, in which, as we have seen, bailiffs were sometimes killed. At another time some aggrieved tradesmen who resisted the tolls demanded by the authorities on his industry of gin or gingerbread selling, would provide the mob with a chance of asserting themselves and defying the authorities. Their operations would then add an attraction to the fair which was much appreciated by large numbers of its patrons. When such incidents failed, the mere breaking of a swing-boat was excuse enough for the burning of the entire apparatus, and for an organized expedition throughout the precincts of the carnival in search of similar erections, and a general conflagration followed, in which the benches and tables of the sausage vendors were added to the flames. Altogether, however, there is very little record of loss of life or damage to property in connection with the fair during its vogue of five centuries. A stage broke down occasionally when the piety of Noah or King Solomon, or the wings of the angels or the godhead of Apollo or Jupiter, failed to save them from broken limbs. A juggler or a tight-rope dancer paid with his life for his courage and temerity on occasion. But disaster was rare, and the fact that a congregation of such inflammable material as mustered annually in Smithfield escaped serious fire is a standing wonder to this day.

from Amusements of Old London by W. J. Boulton

At His Majesty's Bear Garden at Hockley in the Hole, this present Monday, three great matches will be fought.

First, a brindled dog from Hampstead to fight against a fallow-coloured bitch from Chelsea; to fight ten let goes apiece at the famous Newington Bull for half a guinea each; the dog or bitch which goes farthest in or fairest, wins the money.

Secondly, a fallow-coloured dog from Whitechapel to fight against a fallow-coloured from Spittlefields Market, both to fight let go for let go at the famous Cambridge Bull for one guinea each, the dog that is killed or runs away, loses the money.

Likewise, a mad bull to be dressed up with fireworks and turned loose in the game-place.

Likewise, a dog to be dressed up with fireworks over him and turned loose with the bull amongst the men in the ground, also a bear to be turned loose at the same time, and a cat to be ty'd to the bull's tail.

Note:– The doors will be open at four and the sport begin between five and six o'clock, because the diversion will last long and the days grow short.

As late as 1815, Hampstead was still a country village. The suburban sprawl had not started:

A steeple issuing from a leafy rise,
   With farmy fields in front and sloping green,
   Dear Hampstead, is thy southern face serene,
Silently smiling on approaching eyes,
Within, thine ever-shifting looks surprise,
   Streets, hills and dells, trees overhead now seen,
   Now down below, with smoking roofs between, –
A village, revelling in varieties.
Then northward what a range – with heath and pond!
   Nature's own ground; woods that let mansions through
And cottaged vales with billowy fields beyond,
   And clump of darkening pines, and prospects blue,
And that clear path through all, where daily meet
Cool cheeks, and brilliant eyes, and morn-elastic feet!

Leigh Hunt

Old and New London

22

London Grows

The Industrial Revolution also brought phenomenal growth to London. Immigrants poured into the city from a depressed countryside. "The Great Wen", Cobbett called London:

[ONE had only] to look at the face of the country, including [the] Wen [of London], to behold the effects of taking property from one man and giving it to another. The monstrous streets and squares, and circuits, and crescents, the pulling down of streets and building up new ones; the making of bridges and tunnels, till the Thames itself trembled at the danger of being marched and undermined: the everlasting ripping-up of pavements and the tumblings up of the earth to form drains and sewers, till all beneath us was like a honeycomb. [One had only] to look at the thousands employed in cracking the stones upon the highways, while the docks and thistles and couchgrass were choking the land on the other side of the hedges; to see England, land of plenty and never-ending stores, without an old wheat rick, and with not more than a stock of two-thirds the former cattle upon the farms: to see the troops of half-starved creatures flocking from the fields, and, in their smock-frocks and nailed shoes, begging their way up to [the cities], in order to get a chance snap at the crumbs and the orts rejected by idleness and luxury—of all the destructive things that could fall upon a nation; of all the horrid curses that could afflict it, none was equal to that of robbing productive labour of its reward, of taking from the industrious and giving to the idle.

from *Autobiography* by William Cobbett

Later, in 1847, Lord Shaftesbury wrote of the same immigration; and the cheap lodging houses that were the first resorts of the poor:

More of rustic innocence and honest purpose, both in males and females, has suffered shipwreck in these *lodging-houses* than from any other perils that try the skill and courage of young adventurers . . . . The stonishment and perplexities of a young person on his arrival here, full of good intentions to live honestly, would be almost ludicrous, were they not the prelude to such mournful

results. He alights—and is instantly directed, for the best accommodation, to Duck Lane, St Gile's, Saffron Hill, Spitalfields or
Whitechapel. He reaches the indicated region through tight avenues
of glittering fish and rotten vegetables, with doorways or alleys
gaping on either side—which, if they be not choked with squalid
garments or sickly children, lead the eye through an almost
interminable vista of filth and distress . . . The pavement, where
there is any, is bespattered with dirt of every hue, ancient enough to
rank with the fossils, but offensive as the most recent deposits. The
houses, small, low, and mournful, present no one part, in windows,
door-posts, or brickwork, that seems fitted to stand for another
week—rags and hurdles stuff up the panes, and defend the passages
blackened with use and by the damps arising from the undrained
and ill-ventilated recesses. Yet each one affects to smile with
promise, and invites the country-bumpkin to the comfort and
repose of "Lodgings for single men".

Poverty and Slum living, c. 1870

The old city had always been overcrowded. Now it could no longer cope and London burst outwards. The sprawl of suburbs was helped by the building of railways. To commerce, the main lines brought prosperity; to the engineers a creative excitement. Brunel writes about Paddington Station:

I am going to design, in a great hurry, and I believe to build, a Station after my own fancy; that is, with engineering roofs, etc., etc. It is at Paddington, in a cutting, and admitting of no exterior, all interior and all roofed in. Now, such a thing will be entirely *metal* as to all the general forms, arrangements and design; it almost of necessity becomes an Engineering Work, but, to be honest, even if it were not, it is a brand of architecture of which I am fond, and, *of course*, believe myself fully competent for; but for *detail* of ornamentation I neither have time nor knowledge, and with all my confidence in my own ability I have never any objection to advice and assistance even in the department which I keep to myself, namely the general design.

Now, in this building which, *entre nous*, will be one of the largest of its class, I want to carry out, strictly and fully, all those correct notions of the use of metal which I believe you and I share (except that I should carry them still farther than you) and I think it will be a nice opportunity.

from a letter by Isambard Kingdom Brunel to Digby Wyatt,
January 13th 1851

Paddington Station

Berkhampstead Station

The Railroad comes. . . . .

The first shock of a great earthquake had, just at that period, rent
the whole neighbourhood to its centre. Traces of its course were
visible on every side. Houses were knocked down; streets broken
through and stopped; deep pits and trenches dug in the ground;
enormous heaps of earth and clay thrown up; buildings that were
undermined and shaking, propped by great beams of wood. Here
a chaos of carts, overthrown and jumbled together, lay topsy-turvy
at the bottom of a steep unnatural hill; there, confused treasures of
iron soaked and rusted in something that had accidentally become a
pond. Everywhere were bridges that led nowhere; thoroughfares
that were wholly impassable; Babel towers of chimneys, wanting
half their height; temporary wooden houses and enclosures, in the
most unlikely situations; carcases of ragged tenements, and frag-
ments of unfinished walls and arches, and piles of scaffolding, and
wildernesses of bricks, and giant forms of cranes, and tripods stradd-
ling above nothing. There were a hundred thousand shapes and
substances of incompleteness, wildly mingled out of their places,
upside down, burrowing in the earth, aspiring in the air, mouldering
in the water, and unintelligible as any dream. Hot springs and fiery

eruptions, the usual attendants upon earthquakes, lent their contributions of confusion to the scene. Boiling water hissed and heaved within dilapidated walls; whence, also, the glare and roar of flames came issuing forth; and mounds of ashes blocked up rights of way, and wholly changed the law and custom of the neighbourhood.

In short, the yet unfinished and unopened Railroad was in progress; and, from the very core of all this dire disorder, trailed smoothly away, upon its mighty course of civilization and improvement.

But as yet, the neighbourhood was shy to own the Railroad. One or two bold speculators had projected streets; and one had built a little, but had stopped among the mud and ashes to consider farther of it. A bran-new Tavern, redolent of fresh mortar and size, and fronting nothing at all, had taken for its sign The Railway Arms; but that might be rash enterprise—and then it hoped to sell drink to the workmen. So, the Excavators' House of Call had sprung up from a beer-shop; and the old-established Ham and Beef Shop had become the Railway Eating House, with a roast leg of pork daily, through interested motives of a similar immediate and popular description. Lodging-house keepers were favourable in like manner; and for the like reasons were not to be trusted. The general belief was very slow.

Later. . . . .

The miserable waste ground, where the refuse-matter had been heaped of yore, was swallowed up and gone; and in its frowsy stead were tiers of warehouses, crammed with rich goods and costly merchandise. The old by-streets now swarmed with passengers and vehicles of every kind: the new streets that had stopped disheartened in the mud and waggon-ruts, formed towns within themselves, originating wholesome comforts and conveniences belonging to themselves, and never tried nor thought of until they sprung into existence. Bridges that had led to nothing, led to villas, gardens, churches, healthy public walks. The carcases of houses, and beginnings of new thoroughfares, had started off upon the line at steam's own speed, and shot away into the country in a monster train.

As to the neighbourhood which had hesitated to acknowledge the Railroad in its straggling days, that had grown wise and penitent, as any Christian might in such a case, and now boasted of its powerful and prosperous relation. There were railway patterns in its drapers' shop and railway journals in the windows of its newsmen. There were railway hotels, office-houses, lodging-houses, boarding-houses; railway plans, maps, views, wrappers, bottles, sandwich-boxes, and time-tables; railway hackey-coach and cabstands; railway omnibuses, railway streets and buildings, railway hangers-on and parasites, and flatterers out of all calculation. There was even railway time observed in clocks, as if the sun itself had given in. Among the vanquished was the master chimney-sweeper, who now lived in a stuccoed house three stories high, and gave himself out, with golden flourishes upon a varnished board, as contractor for the cleansing of railway chimneys by machinery.

To and from the heart of this great change, all day and night, throbbing currents rushed and returned incessantly like its life's blood. Crowds of people and mountains of goods, departing and arriving scores upon scores of times in every four-and-twenty hours, produced a fermentation in the place that was always in action. The very houses seemed disposed to pack up and take trips.

from *Dombey and Son* by Charles Dickens

In 1830, the Armstrongs decided to move out of London:

It was thought advisable to take some small place in the country for the benefit of our health . . . (My father) took a very pretty and rather commodious cottage-residence at Southall Green, Middlesex, about a mile out of the high road to Uxbridge, and exactly ten miles from Tyburn Gate. Our intention was to reside half the year at Southall, and the remainder in London, and I remember we moved there on the 26th June 1830. My delight at everything I saw was beyond bounds—gardens were allotted my sister and self—there was the canal to fish in—a pony to ride—besides animals of different kinds. Having been long pent up in town, Annie and myself viewed Southall as a second Paradise, and I remember I nearly hung myself on my pin-before the very first morning after our arrival, in attempting to scale the yard gates to see the country beyond them.

Later, the railway line from Paddington arrived:

A remarkable change for the worse took place about this time in the hitherto retired neighbourhood of Southall Green. The railway spread dissatisfaction and immorality among the poor, the place being inundated with worthless and overpaid navigators; the very appearance of the countryside was altered, some families left, and the rusticity of the village gave place to a London-out-of-town character. Moss-grown cottages retired before new ones with bright red tiles, picturesque hedgerows were succeeded by prim iron railings, and the village inn, once a pretty cottage with a swinging sign, is transmogrified to the "Railway Tavern" with an intimation gaudily set forth that "London porter" and other luxuries hitherto unknown to the aborigines were to be procured within.

from *English Social History* by G. M. Trevelyan

How the City Spreads

The second home is on the other side of London, near to where the busy great north road of bygone days is silent and almost deserted, except by wayfarers who toil along on foot. It is a poor small house, barely and sparely furnished, but very clean; and there is even an attempt to decorate it, shown in the homely flowers trained about the porch and in the narrow garden. The neighbourhood in which it stands has as little of the country to recommend it, as it has of the town. It is neither of the town nor country. The former, like the giant in his travelling boots, has made a stride and passed it, and has set his brick-and-mortar heel a long way in advance; but the intermediate space between the giant's feet, as yet, is only blighted country, and not town; and, here, among a few tall chimneys belching smoke all day and night, and among the brick-fields and the lanes where turf is cut, and where the fences tumble down, and where the dusty nettles grow, and where a scrap or two of hedge may be seen, and where the bird-catcher still comes occasionally, though he swears every time to come no more—this second home is to be found.

from *Dombey and Son* by Charles Dickens

Park Village East, Regent's Park

City of the Rich

It was now summer-time, a grey, hot, dusty evening. They rode to the top of Oxford Street, and there alighting, dived in among the great streets of melancholy stateliness, and the little streets that try to be as stately and succeed in being more melancholy, of which there is a labyrinth near Park Lane. Wildernesses of corner houses, with barbarous old porticoes and appurtenances; horrors that came into existence under some wrong-headed person in some wrong-headed time, still demanding the blind admiration of all ensuing generations and determined to do so until they tumbled down; frowned upon the twilight. Parasite little tenements, with the cramp in their whole frame, from the dwarf hall-door on the giant model of His Grace's in the Square to the squeezed window of the boudoir commanding the dunghills in the Mews, made the evening doleful. Rickety dwellings of undoubted fashion, but of a capacity to hold nothing comfortably except a dismal smell, looked like the last result of the great mansions' breeding in-and-in; and, where their little supplementary bows and balconies were supported on thin iron columns, seemed to be scrofulously resting upon crutches. Here and there a Hatchment, with the whole science of Heraldry in it, loomed down upon the street, like an Archbishop discoursing on Vanity. The shops, few in number, made no show; for popular opinion was as nothing to them. The pastrycook knew who was on his books, and in that knowledge could be calm, with a few glass cylinders of dowager peppermint-drops in his window, and half-a-dozen ancient specimens of currant-jelly. A few oranges formed the greengrocer's whole concession to the vulgar mind. A single basket made of moss, once containing plovers' eggs, held all that the poulterer had to say to the rabble. Everybody in those streets seemed (which is always the case at that hour and season) to be gone out to dinner, and nobody seemed to be giving the dinners they had gone to. On the doorsteps there were lounging footmen with bright parti-coloured plumage and white polls, like an extinct race of monstrous birds; and butlers, solitary men of recluse demeanour, each of whom appeared distrustful of all the other butlers. The roll of carriages in the Park was done for the day; the street lamps were lighting; and wicked little grooms in the tightest fitting garments, with twists in their legs answering to the twists in their minds, hung about in pairs, chewing straws and exchanging fraudulent secrets. The spotted dogs who went out with the carriages, and who were so associated with splendid equipages that it looked like a condescension in those animals to come out without them, accompanied helpers to and fro on messages. Here and there was a retiring public-house which did not require to be supported on the shoulders of the people, and where gentlemen out of livery were not much wanted.

*　*　*　*　*

Upon that establishment of state, the Merdle establishment in Harley Street, Cavendish Square, there was the shadow of no more common wall than the fronts of other establishments of state on the opposite side of the street. Like unexceptionable Society, the opposing rows of houses in Harley Street were very grim with one another. Indeed, the mansions and their inhabitants were so much alike in that respect, that the people were often to be found drawn up on opposite sides of dinner-tables, in the shade of their own loftiness, staring at the other side of the way with the dulness of the houses.

Everybody knows how like the street, the two dinner-rows of people who take their stand by the street will be. The expressionless uniform twenty houses, all to be knocked at and rung at in the same form, all approachable by the same dull steps, all fended off by the pattern of railing, all with the same impracticable fire-escapes, the same inconvenient fixtures in their heads, and everything without exception to be taken at a high valuation—who had not dined with these? The house so drearily out of repair, the occasional bow-window, the stuccoed house, the newly-fronted house, the corner house with nothing but angular rooms, the house with the blinds always down, the house with the hatchment always up, the house where the collector has called for one quarter of an Idea, and found nobody at home—who has not dined with these? The house that nobody will take, and is to be had a bargain—who does not know her? The showy house that was taken for life by the disappointed gentleman, and which does not suit him at all—who is unacquainted with that haunted habitation?

Harley Street, Cavendish Square, was more than aware of Mr and

Mrs Merdle. Intruders there were in Harley Street, of whom it was not aware; but Mr and Mrs Merdle it delighted to honour. Society was aware of Mr and Mrs Merdle. Society had said "Let us license them; let us know them".

Mr Merdle was immensely rich; a man of prodigious enterprise; a Midas without the ears, who turned all he touched to gold. He was in everything good, from banking to building. He was in Parliament, of course. He was in the City, necessarily. He was Chairman of this, Trustee of that, President of the other. The weightiest of men had said to projectors, "Now, what name have you got? Have you got Merdle?" And, the reply being in the negative, had said "Then I won't look at you."

from *Little Dorrit* by Charles Dickens

The Stock Exchange

The Great Exhibition

The outward sign of prosperity in mid-century was the Great Exhibition in Hyde Park. Paxton designed the Crystal Palace of metal and glass; Brunel was on the Exhibition committee.

Cover of the catalogue for the Great Exhibition of 1851

This day is one of the greatest & most glorious days of our lives, with which, to my pride & joy the name of my dearly beloved Albert is forever associated! It is a day which makes my heart swell with thankfulness! The Park presented a wonderful spectacle, crowds streaming through it,—carriages & troops passing, quite like the Coronation Day, & for *me*, the same anxiety. The day was bright, & all bustle & excitement. At ½ p. 11, the whole procession in 9 state carriages, was set in motion. Vicky & Bertie were in our carriage. Vicky was dressed in lace over white satin, with a small wreath of pink wild roses, in her hair, & looked very nice. Bertie was in full Highland dress. The Green Park & Hyde Park were one mass of densely crowded human beings, in the highest good humour & most enthusiastic. I never saw Hyde Park look as it did, being filled with crowds as far as the eye could reach. A little rain fell, just as we started; but before we neared the Crystal Palace, the sun shone & gleamed upon the gigantic edifice, upon which the flags of every nation were flying. We drove up Rotten Row & got out of our carriages at the entrance on that side. The glimpse through the iron gates of the Transept, the moving palms & flowers, the myriads of people filling the galleries & seats around, together with the flourish of trumpets, as we entered the building, gave a sensation I shall never forget, & I felt much moved. We went for a moment into a little room where we left our cloaks & found Mama & Mary. Outside all the Princes were standing. In a few seconds we proceeded, Albert leading me having Vicky at his hand, & Bertie holding mine. The sight as we came to the centre where the steps & chair (on which I did not sit) was placed, facing the beautiful crystal fountain was magic & impressive. The tremendous cheering, the joy expressed in every face, the vastness of the building, with all its decorations & exhibits, the sound of the organ (with 200 instruments & 600 voices, which seemed nothing), & my beloved Husband the creator of this great "Peace Festival", uniting the industry & art of *all* nations of the earth, *all* this, was indeed moving, & a day to live forever. God bless my dearest Albert, & my dear Country which has shown itself so great today.

from Queen Victoria's Journal for May 1st 1851

The Crystal Palace

Contraption,—that's the bizarre, proper slang,
Eclectic word, for this portentous toy,
The flying-machine, that gyrates stiffly, arms
A-kimbo, so to say, and baskets slung
From every elbow, skating in the air.
Irreverent, we; but Tartars from Thibet
May deem Sir Hiram the Grandest Lama, deem
His volatile machinery best, and most
Magnific, rotatory engine, meant
For penitence and prayer combined, whereby
Petitioner as well as orison
Are spun about in space: a solemn rite
Before the portal of that fane unique,
Victorian temple of commercialism,
Our very own eighth wonder of the world
The Crystal Palace.

But come: here's crowd; here's mod; a gala day!
The walks are black with people: no one hastes;
They all pursue their purpose business-like—
The polo-ground, the cycle-track; but most
Invade the palace glumly once again.
It is 'again'; you feel it in the air—
Resigned habitués on every hand:
And yet agog; abandoned, yet concerned!
They can't tell why they come; they only know
They must shove through the holiday somehow.

In the main floor the fretful multitude
Circulates from the north nave to the south
Across the central transept—swish and tread
And murmur, like a seaboard's mingled sound.
About the sideshows eddies swirl and swing:
Distorting mirrors; waltzing-tops—wherein
Couples are wildly spun contrariwise
To your revolving platforms; biographs,
Or rifle-ranges; panoramas: choose!

As stupid as it was last holiday?
They think so,—every whit! Outside, perhaps?
A spice of danger in the flying-machine?
A few who passed that whirligig, their hopes
On higher things, return disconsolate
To try the Tartar's volant oratory.
Others again, no more anticipant
Of any active business in their own
Diversion, joining stalwart folk who sought
At once the polo-ground, the cycle-track,
Accept the ineludible; while some
(Insidious anti-climax here) frequent
The water-entertainments—shallops, chutes
And rivers subterrene:—thus, passive, all,
Like savages bewitched, submit at last
To be the dupes of pleasure, sadly gay—
Victims, and not companions, of delight!

John Davidson

The Great Exhibition—Hardware Department

Commemoration of The

GREAT REVOLUTIONARY MOVEMENTS OF 1848
ALLIANCE OF ALL PEOPLES

An
international
soirée
followed by
A Public Meeting
will be held at
St. Martin's Hall
Long Acre
on
Tuesday, February 27, 1855

The following distinguished representatives of European Democracy have been invited:

FRENCH: Louis Blanc, Victor Hugo, Barbès, Felix Pyat, Ledru-Rollin, Raspail, Eugène Sue, Pierre Leroux.
GERMAN: Kinkel, Marx, Ruge, Schapper.
ITALIAN: Bianciani, Saffi, Mazzini.
HUNGARIAN: Teleki, Kossuth.
POLISH: Worcell Zeno-Swientoslawski.
RUSSIAN: Herzen.
ENGLISH: W. Coningham, J. Finlen, Cooper, Mayne-Reid, J. Beal, Gerald Massey.

Ernest Jones, President.
Alfred Tallandier, French Sec.
Dombrovski, Polish Sec.
M. Bley, German Sec.
B. Chapman, English Sec.

Tea on Table at Five. Doors open for meeting at half-past Seven, to commence at Eight.

Double Tickets, 2s. 6d.; Single ditto, 1s. 6d.; meeting ditto, 3d.
Tickets may be had at St. Martin's Hall.

London wears a dismal exterior to the eye of the foreigner, because all London is hard at work. The State Secretary in his severely-appointed room, receiving a deputation, has a hard-worked appearance, and looks dressed for downright business. In the clubs, men split into groups, and are all, or nearly all, intent on some weighty affair of the day. The streets West as well as here in the East, where we are being hustled on our way to the Docks, are filled with people who have errands. They are not sad men and women: but they are seriously devoted to the thing in hand. This morning, in the West, young peers—heirs to fat slices of counties—are in the throng, repairing to committee sittings, public meetings, board appointments. Old men, retired from business, are nevertheless going to business. "Better rub than rust." That is a duke, with the bundle of papers under his arm. Here is a member of Parliament, with his documents for the long day and night of work before him, in a bag. Many of the pale figures in wig and gown, pacing Westminster Hall, are slaves to fashionable society, as well as barristers in large practice—and sit up studying their briefs after the rout is over. Their luncheon is in a sandwich box; so that Nature's cravings may not rob them of an hour in the best part of the precious working time in the West. The ordinary daily labours of a City alderman, who is in business as well as on the bench, would fill the week of an Italian—and leave him exhausted on the seventh day. There is not a happier man than this same alderman; and his content is never so hearty as when he is marching from one duty to another. His features are set—his manner is solid. He looks into no shop—heeds no passer-by. Directness is his quality—it is that also of the crowds threading their ways swiftly on all sides. Energy and earnestness pervade London shops—and are of fiery intensity in the popular markets. Take the Whitechapel Road on a Saturday night, or Camden Town, or Knightsbridge, or the Borough, or Tottenham Court Road: the vehemence of the street traders is alarming to a stranger, who anticipates a score of cases of apoplexy. St Martin's-le-Grand, when the boxes are about to close! The Docks, when the wind has wafted a fleet home from the Downs! Or, Petticoat Lane on Sunday morning! Or Billingsgate, when the market opens! Here, emphatically, I repeat, is London!

And in no part of London does Work wear more changing, more picturesque phases than in the narrow, tortuous, river-side street, that leads from the quiet of the Temple to the Tower—and so, on to the docks. In this river-side thoroughfare there are more varieties of business activity than in any other I can call to mind. Glimpses of the Thames to the left, through tangles of chains, and shafts, and ropes, and cranes; and to the right crowded lanes, with bales and boxes swinging at every height in the air, and waggon-loads of merchandise waiting to be warehoused: and, in the stately water way, confined in granite walls and flanked by groves and gardens. At least, let us hope so; for there is economy in greenery, in a city like London. . . .

The view immediately to the west of London Bridge is a many-sided one. The whole round of modern commercial life is massed in the foreground, and the mighty dome which dominates London, swells proudly over the hum, and hiss, and plashing, and whistling, and creaking of the hastening crowds. The bales are swinging in the air; files of dingy people are passing into the steam-boats; the sleepy barges lower masts to pass the bridges; the heavy traffic between the City and the Borough is dragging over Southwark Bridge; trains glide across the railway arches into the prodigious Canon Street shed. Factories, warehouses, mills, works; barges, wherries, skiffs, tugs, penny-boats; smoke and steam blurring all; and the heaving water churned from its bed and feverish in its ebb and flow—have a grandeur that enlivens the imagination. A little pulse of the mighty organization is laid bare. It is an eddy in the turbulent stream of London life. It is eminently suggestive of the activity that is behind the wharves, and landing-stages, and mills.

from *London—a Pilgrimage* by Doré and Jerrold

*   *   *   *   *

The Working City

Before six in the morning, while the mantle of night still lies over the sloppy streets, and the air stings the limbs to the marrow, the shadows of men and boys may be seen, black objects against the deep gloom, gliding out of the side-streets to the main thoroughfares. They are the vanguard of the army of Labour, who are to carry forward the marvellous story of London industry another step before sundown: to add a new story to a new terrace; the cornerstone to another building; bulwarks to another frigate; another station to another railway; and tons upon tons of produce from every clime, to the mighty stock that is for ever packed along the shores of the Thames. As they trudge on their way, the younger and lighter-hearted whistling defiance to the icy wind, the swift carts of fishmongers, butchers, and greengrocers pass them; and they meet the slow-returning waggons of the market-gardeners, with the men asleep upon the empty baskets. The baked-potato man and the keeper of the coffee-stall are their most welcome friends—and their truest; for they sell warmth that sustains and does not poison.

As the day breaks, in winter, the suburbs become alive with shop-boys and shop-men, poor clerks, needlewomen of quick and timorous gait, and waiters who have to prepare for the day. The night cabs are crawling home; and the day cabs are being horsed in the steamy mews. The milkmen and women are abroad—first street vocalists of the day. The early omnibus draws up outside the public-house, the bar of which has just been lit up. The barmaid serves sharp of temper and short in word—in her curl papers. The blinds creep up the windows of the villas. The news-boys shamble along, laden with the morning papers; prodigal of chaff, and profuse in the exhibition of comforters. The postman's knock rings through the street; and at the sound every man who has to labour for his bread—whether banker, banker's clerk, porter, or vendor of fusees at the bank entrance—is astir.

Another working day has fairly opened; and mighty and multi-form is the activity. Hasty making of tea and coffee, filling of shaving pots, brushing of boots and coats and hats, reading of papers, opening of morning letters, kissing of wives and daughters,

Early morning in Covent Garden Market

grasping of reins, mounting of omnibuses, and catching of trains—
in every suburb! The start has been made: and the sometime silent
City is filling at a prodigious rate. The trim omnibuses from
Clapham and Fulham, from Hackney and Hampstead, make a
valiant opposition to the suburban lines of railway. The bridges are
choked with vehicles. While the City is being flooded with money-
making humanity, the West End streets are given up to shop-cleaners
and town travellers; and while these early bread-winners are pre-
paring for the fashion of the day, gentlemen who live at ease, amble
to and fro the early burst in the park; and Her Majesty's civil
servants honour the pavement, each looking as though he had just
stepped out of a band-box, and protested somewhat at the stern duty
that compelled him to emerge before the day was aired—to use
Beau Brummell's delightfully whimsical phrase.

On our way to the City on the tide of Labour, we light upon places
in which the day is never aired: only the high points of which the sun
ever hits. Rents spread with rags, swarming with children of mothers

for ever greasing the walls with their shoulders; where there is an angry hopelessness and carelessness painted upon the face of every man and woman; and the oaths are loud, and the crime is continuous; and the few who do work with something like system, are the ne'er do weels of the great army. As the sun rises, the court swarms at once: for here there are no ablutions to perform, no toilettes to make—neither brush nor comb delays the outpouring of babes and sucklings from the cellars and garrets. And yet in the midst of such a scene as this we cannot miss touches of human goodness, and of honourable instinct making a tooth-and-nail fight against adverse circumstances. Some country wenches, who have been cast into London—Irish girls mostly—hasten out of the horrors of the common lodging-house to market, where they buy their flowers, for the day's huckstering in the City. They are to be seen selling roses and camellias, along the kerb by the Bank, to dapper clerks. There is an affecting expression in the faces of some of these rough *bouquetières*, that speaks of honourable effort to make headway out of the lodging-house and the rents; and reminds one of Hood's Peggy rather than of the bold, daintily attired damsel who decorated the button-holes of the Paris Jockey Club under the Empire. Then there are sad, lonely, unclassed men, who are striving might and main to keep out of the lowest depths: widowers left with sickly children; small tradesmen who have been ruined, and are not fit for rough unskilled work; even men of superior station—as worn-out, unfortunate clerks or schoolmasters. Some, in their very despair, beg; others become hireling scribes for their low associates; others, again, fall ultimately out of the lists of labour—whether honest or dishonest—and are carried off, protesting to the last, to the House. Some—of merrier mood—take to trifle-selling in the streets.

Waking London is, indeed, a wonderful place to study, from the park where the fortunate in the world's battle are gathering roses, to the stone-yard by Shadwell where, at day-break one chilly morning, we saw the houseless, who had had a crust and a shake-down in the casual ward, turn to the dreary labour by which it was to be paid.

from London—a Pilgrimage by Doré and Jerrold

Behind the Facade

I was anxious to see the room in which the gang of boy crossing-sweepers lived, so that I might judge of their peculiar style of house-keeping, and form some notion of their principles of domestic economy.

I asked young Harry and "the Goose" to conduct me to their lodgings, and they at once consented, "the Goose" prefacing his compliance with the remark, that "it weren't such a genilmen had been accustomed to, but then I must take 'em as they was".

The boys led me in the direction of Drury-lane; and before entering one of the narrow streets which branch off like the side-bones of a fish's spine from that long thoroughfare, they thought fit to caution me that I was not to be frightened, as nobody would touch me, for all was very civil.

The locality consisted of one of those narrow streets which, were it not for the paved cartway in the centre, would be called a court. Seated on the pavement at each side of the entrance was a coster-woman with her basket before her, and her legs tucked up mysteriously under her gown into a round ball, so that her figure resembled in shape the plaster tumblers sold by the Italians. These women remained as inanimate as if they had been carved images, and it was only when a passenger went by they gave signs of life, by calling out in a low voice, like talking to themselves, "Two for three haarpence—herrens,"—"Fine hinguns."

The street itself is like the description given of thoroughfares in the East. Opposite neighbours could not exactly shake hands out of window, but they could talk together very comfortably; and indeed, as I passed along, I observed several women with their arms folded like a cat's paws on the sill, and chatting with their friends over the way.

Nearly all the inhabitants were costermongers, and, indeed, the narrow cartway seemed to have been made just wide enough for a truck to wheel down it. A beershop and a general store, together with a couple of sweeps—whose residences were distinguished by a broom over the door—formed the only exceptions to the street-selling class of inhabitants.

As I entered the place, it gave me the notion that it belonged to a

44

district coster colony, and formed one large hawkers' home for everybody seemed to be doing just as he liked, and I was stared at as if considered an intruder. Women were seated on the pavement, knitting, and repairing their linen; the doorways were filled up with bonnetless girls, who wore their shawls over their heads, as the Spanish women do their mantillas; and the youths in corduroy and brass buttons, who were chatting with them, leant against the walls as they smoked their pipes, and blocked up the pavement, as if they were the proprietors of the place. Little children formed a convenient bench out of the kerbstone; and a party of four men were seated on the footway, playing with cards which had turned to the colour of brown paper from long usage, and marking the points with chalk upon the flags.

The parlour-windows of the houses had all of them wooden shutters, as thick and clumsy-looking as a kitchen flap-table, the paint of which had turned to the dull dirt-colour of an old slate. Some of these shutters were evidently never used as a security for the dwelling, but served only as tables on which to chalk the accounts of the day's sales.

Before most of the doors were costermonger's trucks—some standing ready to be wheeled off, and others stained and muddy with the day's work. A few of the costers were dressing up their barrows, arranging the sieves of waxy-looking potatoes—and others taking the stiff herrings, browned like a meerschaum with the smoke they had been dried in, from the barrels beside them, and spacing them out in pennyworths on their trays.

You might guess what each costermonger had taken out that day by the heap of refuse swept into the street before the doors. One house had a blue mound of mussel-shells in front of it—another, a pile of the outside leaves of broccoli and cabbages, turning yellow and slimy with bruises and moisture.

Hanging up beside some of the doors were bundles of old strawberry pottles, stained red with the fruit. Over the trap-doors to the cellars were piles of market-gardeners' sieves, ruddled like a sheep's back with big red letters. In fact, everything that met the eye seemed to be in some way connected with the coster's trade.

From the windows poles stretched out, on which blankets, petticoats, and linen were drying; and so numerous were they, that they reminded me of the flags hung out at a Paris fête. Some of the sheets had patches as big as trap-doors let into their centres; and the blankets were—many of them—as full of holes as a pigeon-house.

As I entered the court, a "row" was going on; and from a first-floor window a lady, whose hair sadly wanted brushing, was haranguing a crowd beneath, throwing her arms about like a drowning man, and in her excitement thrusting her body half out of her temporary rostrum as energetically as I have seen Punch lean over his theatre.

"The willin dragged her," she shouted, "by the hair of her head, at least three yards into the court—the willin! and then he kicked her, and the blood was on his boot."

from *London Labour and the London Poor* by Henry Mayhew

Slum London, 1889

Goldsmith Street

This street, formerly "The Coal Yard", lies parallel to Macklin Street, opening out of Drury Lane, but instead of reaching through to Newton Street it turns at right angles and debouches in Macklin Street. At the corner in Macklin Street stands the mortuary, and behind it reaching back some distance with blank wall to Goldsmith Street are some parish almshouses, of which the entrance is in Macklin Street, between Nos. 17 and 19. The building now used for these almshouses was originally St Giles's Round-house, an old detached fabric built, as its name imports, in a cylindrical form, but it had undergone from time to time so many alterations that its symmetry was destroyed and its walls bulging made it resemble an enormous cask, a resemblance which was increased by the small circular aperture which served for a door pierced like a bunghole in its side at some distance from the ground. This was approached by a flight of wooden steps. The prison was two storeys high, with a flat roof surmounted by a gilt vane fashioned like a key. There was considerable accommodation inside, and it had in its day accommodated many thousands of disorderly persons. In this Round-house it is said that Jonathan Wild and Jack Sheppard were in their turn locked up, and from it they succeeded in escaping. The building which was erected in 1790, was finally given to the Almshouse authorities of St Giles's-in-the-Fields and St George's, Bloomsbury, for the residence of twenty poor women of these parishes, and was rebuilt in 1885. The rest of this portion of Goldsmith Street, occupied by business premises, was formerly the site of Barley Court and always full of girls and base women who could do any diabolical work. Once they threw a man out of window and killed him. Just at the back of this court stood the matron's house of the new almshouses, and in the midst of such vice and wretchedness the poor old ladies lived. Of the same character were four houses of three rooms each which stood at the corner where the street turns towards Drury Lane. They too are gone, and business premises stand in their place. Proceeding along Goldsmith Street towards Drury Lane one crosses Smart's Buildings, and on the south side, where now stands the Board School, there was a peculiar place called the Galleries. Some houses two storeys high occupied by bad women faced the street, but at back was a large space of ground. This was built round and a single door was the only entrance. The ground floors of these buildings were used for stabling costers' donkeys, and above were rooms in which dwelt a rough, desperate class of Irish costers and others. One of these visited by my informant was a rat-catcher, his room full of boxes of ferrets and surly dogs. The man was as surly as his dogs and as sharp as his ferrets, and as rough a customer as any rat; his wife, a meek quiet woman, lived to do his bidding and kept the place as clean as it might be.

At the Drury Lane end on the south side of Goldsmith Street are a carpenter's shop and dairy, and beyond the dairy are the cow-sheds. The dairyman lives at the dairy, but no one now resides at the carpenter's shop. Opposite on the north corner stand "Goldsmith's Buildings", a model block accommodating thirty families, mostly costers too newly come for individual details to be given; they are mostly second-class costers, employed by others to hawk round cheap commodities. Onward the houses bear regular numbers from 3 upwards. *Nos. 3* and *5* are occupied by a family who have prospered wonderfully. Its members divide, some going into the country, where they collect moss, ferns, etc., or buy flowers, which are sent home by train and sold in Covent Garden market. Others do this on a smaller scale and single-handed, going out a few miles from London by train or tramping on foot if they have no money, to collect groundsell or chickweed for birds, or creeping-Jenny and sprays of ivy, which, coming back next day, they sell in the streets.

At *No. 7* lives a car-man in broken-down health. He fell off his cart and being run over broke his leg. On the floor above is a very poor old lady living on charity, but a happy soul expectant of heaven. . . .

Nos. 11, 13, and *15* contain each nine or ten families, mostly fond of drink and poor. Many of these belong to the coster class. . . . *No. 23,* the corner of Smart's Buildings, is occupied by a prosperous Irishman who deals in fish and fowls. Beyond Smart's Buildings there is a smithy and foundry occupying *Nos. 25* and *27. No. 29* is a double house where lived and died an old man who had saved enough to own some of these houses, but his heirs have sold them and spent the money, and now live at top of *No. 30,* where also lives on the lower floor a poor coster. *No. 31* is a stable with rooms over it, occupied by caretaker to parish stone-yard. Where the street turned there was a double house pulled down to make the entrance to the stone-yard, which with the casual wards, reaches to Macklin Street. . . .

This street, long and narrow, presents a very unattractive vista to anyone passing along the main street and looking up. Its length is relieved by only one break where a small street crosses. Walking along it, most of the houses appear poverty-stricken and all have a grimy look. It is the same with the people. Some of them can be counted above the line of poverty, and their poverty seems to be of a dismal, vicious type. All the same their amusement is catered for. A crowd had gathered at the further end of the street round two performers, each of whom in turn did feats of skill and strength while his companion turned the handle of the piano. The crowd consisted of the inhabitants who, it being Saturday afternoon, were hanging about—young and old, male and female. Of passers-by there would be few besides myself.

from *Life and Labour of the People in London: Volume II*
by Charles Booth

William Booth's poster on the lot of the Match Girls

Suburban life was very different:

My dear wife Carrie and I have just been a week in our new house, "The Laurels", Brickfield Terrace, Holloway—a nice six-roomed residence, not counting basement, with a front breakfast-parlour. We have a little front garden; and there is a flight of ten steps up to the front door, which, by-the-by, we keep locked with the chain up. Cummings, Gowing, and our other intimate friends always come to the little side entrance, which saves the servant the trouble of going up to the front door, thereby taking her from her work. We have a nice little back garden which runs down to the railway. We were rather afraid of the noise of the trains at first, but the landlord said we should not notice them after a bit, and took £2 off the rent. He was certainly right; and beyond the cracking of the garden wall at the bottom, we have suffered no inconvenience.

After my work in the City, I like to be at home. What's the good of a home, if you are never in it? "Home, Sweet Home", that's my motto. I am always in of an evening. Our old friend Gowing may drop in without ceremony; so may Cummings, who lives opposite. My dear wife Caroline and I are pleased to see them, if they like to drop in on us. But Carrie and I can manage to pass our evenings together without friends.

from *Diary of a Nobody* by George and Weedon Grossmith

His shop was beautifully kept, with its pyramids of polished apples and oranges, its washed racks of potatoes, and coyly opened sacks of mixed nuts. But he was seldom in it, for he did "the round", and for his round he commanded a small cart covered with a tent-like tarpaulin which made it look like the baby of one of the voortrekker wagons of the Boers. A smart little pony drew it and rising from the shafts over the pony's shoulder was an arch of wood and leather from which hung some small golden bells. My uncle decorated this arch according to the season—daffodils, or sprigs of mimosa, heather, or holly and ivy. It made the loaded cart a festival in itself as it jingled chirpily down the neighbouring streets: it brightened the day, so that the children used to watch for it and follow it, and feed the pony knobs of sugar and stroke its nose and mane, and it got so spoilt that it would not leave certain houses without this fee. It was the same pony, of course, which drew the trap for Uncle on Sunday, and got tethered to our lamp-post for its pains, and there attracted a crowd of little children which Uncle had to go out and shoo away like flies every now and then. For "the round" Uncle Herbert dressed in smart riding breeches and riding boots and bowler hat, which made him even more the gentleman-tradesman.

Another circumstance which made Uncle Herbert specially dear to me was that he lived "off the High Street". At the High Street, the straight monotonous streets of the suburb suddenly stopped. Everything became crooked. Not even the houses were alike. Roofs of stained and lichened tiles fell at conflicting angles, and, with gable-ends and chimney buttresses, grouped themselves in Cézanne-like masses round the old giant elms. There were shops half-hidden behind white columns with sanded areas before them and green tubs of ever-greens to mark their territory. The roads went crooked, and for one part of them the trams had to use a single track and if you rode on the top deck you felt you could shake hands with people in the overhanging bedrooms. Crooked alleyways wound under forests of assorted and ancient chimney pots. Because of the white-fronted shops and golden-sanded areas and little tubs, the High Street had a constant air of sunshine and content about it. It was more than half a mile away, and so I did not visit it often as a little boy, but when I did it was with a heart beating with expectation, as though I was certain to find everything strange and glittering there, and the people proud and happy strangers. Of course, I did not understand that the High Street was the old village which our suburb had engulfed, and that it was beautiful. But I knew that it was very special, and so must Uncle Herbert be to live there.

from *The Boy Down Kitchener Street* by Leslie Paul

"How I wish I were a boy!" Mother caught me saying this aloud one day, and promptly told me that this was a wicked thought. She did not go on to give a reason, but merely insisted that it was splended to be a girl, and with such exuberant enthusiasm that I was quite convinced. My father's slogan was that boys should go everywhere and know everything, and that a girl should stay at home and know nothing. Often the boys must have been sorry for me, and one day when I exclaimed, "How lovely it must be to go on the top of a bus!", Dym first laughed at the idea, and then suddenly said, "I say, Barney, let's take her." Barnholt, of course, was only too ready, and I rushed to get my things on before something could happen to stop us. If I had been asked to a royal ball I couldn't have been more excited.

Inside a bus I had often been with mother when we went to Shoolbred's or Peter Robinson's for a morning's shopping. The bus was a box lined with blue velvet, made to carry five each side, of whom mother declared that the fattest always sat next her and half on her, for she was very small. No air got in, except when the door was opened, for the little windows admitted only some so-called light. Straw on the floor, designed to keep our feet warm, was apt to get very wet and dirty. When the bus started the door was firmly shut, the conductor remaining outside with no visible means of support. Presently he would let down the top of the door, put his head in, and ask, "Any for the Angel?"—or whatever the next stage happened to be. Then fares were handed up to him (no tickets were used), and he made a mark with a stumpy pencil on a yellow sheet. I knew what this sheet was called, because all I could amuse myself with during the journey was to read the directions beseeching the passengers to see that their fares were "duly registered on the waybill at the door". We stopped anywhere, for plenty of passengers rather than rapid progress was the main idea. I reckon that the journey from Islington to the West End took a good deal over an hour. Wedged as we were, it was impossible to see anything out of the tiny windows, and the journey was sheer boredom. What with the lack of air, the jerks of the frequent stops, and the jolting over the stone-paved roads, I was usually too ill to stay the course, and we had to get out some distance before our required shop.

A "knifeboard" omnibus

Mysterious as was the mode of attachment of the conductor, the means of getting onto the top was still more so. From the glimpses I had from inside people disappeared bit by bit, their boots last. Of course no woman ever went up. And now, here was I, going to do it myself!

I rushed up again to the study, all dressed, and Dym surveyed me and said I would do. My outdoor clothes in winter never varied: a hat of real sealskin that stood all weathers and could not wear out, neither could it blow off, for it was fastened round my chin by elastic; my warmth was secured by a "crossover"—a strip of tartan about two yards long that crossed over in front and fastened behind, leaving my arms free. The worst worry in going out were my boots, which came far above the ankle with endless buttons that needed a hook to do them up.

Dym decided that it would be best for us to walk to the little side street not far away, where the "Favourite" buses began their journeys. Here we were able to make the ascent at leisure. Dym went up first, then hung down and pointed out the tiny ledges on which I had to put my feet, stretching out his hands to pull me up, while Barnholt fetched up the rear in case I slipped. On the top was what they called the knifeboard—a raised partition along the middle, with seats each side. How people stuck on to them I couldn't imagine.

But the boys had better designs: they scrambled down on to the seat in front, by the driver, and got me there too. "Come along, Missy," said the driver, who was just settling himself for his journey, and I was safely tucked in between him and Dym, with Barnholt on his other side.

How powerful the horse looked from this point of view, how jolly to hear the chuckings and whoas, and to see the whip flourished about, but only gently touching the horse. "I never whips old Rosy," the driver told me. "She's been with me six years and knows what I want. I use the whip like chatting to her." How pitiable were all the people on foot! How contemptible the passengers who went inside! Barnholt, as look-out man, kept calling my attention to things in the shops, and to people doing mysterious jobs in first-floor windows. One room was a nursery, where a boy was riding on a rocking-horse, and in one garden we passed there was a swing with a boy going very high.

We feared to go the whole length of our twopenny ride in case we should be late for tea, so we asked the driver to pull up for us. In my haste to show him how well I could get off by jumping down to Dym in front I fell right into the muddy street. But no harm was done, and the boys picked me up, and we ran home as fast as we could and slipped in at the back door. There was no hiding my mud, and "Wherever have you been?" cried mother. "Oh, just for a run with the boys, and I fell." This was true enough to pass my conscience. Dym was non-plussed, but Barnholt immediately took up the tale of a fine new shop where they sold cricket-bats and bags and things, and how he had thought it better not to spend the shilling Uncle Alfred had given him. On this wave of virtue my muddy dress was forgotten, and we went in to tea with no further questions asked.

from *A London Child of the Seventies* by M. Vivian Hughes

The Strand of those days . . . was the throbbing heart of the people's essential London. Hedged by a maze of continuous alleys and courts, the Strand was fronted by numbers of little restaurants whose windows vaunted exquisite feeding; taverns, dives, oyster and wine bars, ham and beef shops; and small shops marketing a lively variety of curious or workaday things all standing in rank, shoulder to shoulder, to fill the spaces between its many theatres . . . But the mud! And the noise! And the smell! All these blemishes were [the] mark of [the] horse . . .

The whole of London's crowded wheeled traffic—which in parts of the City was at times dense beyond movement—was dependent on the horse: lorry, wagon, bus, hansom and "growler", and coaches and carriages and private vehicles of all kinds, were appendages to horses. Meredith refers to the "anticipatory stench of its cab-stands" on railway approach to London: but the characteristic aroma—for the nose recognized London with gay excitement—was of stables, which were commonly of three or four storeys with inclined ways zigzagging up the faces of them; [their] middens kept the cast-iron filigree chandeliers that glorified the reception rooms of upper- and lower-middle-class homes throughout London encrusted with dead flies and, in late summer, veiled with jiving clouds of them.

A more assertive mark of the horse was the mud that, despite the activities of a numerous corps of red-jacketed boys who dodged among wheels and hooves with pan and brush in service to iron bins at the pavement-edge, either flooded the streets with churnings of "pea soup" that at times collected in pools over-brimming the kerbs, and at others covered the road-surface as with axle grease or bran-laden dust to the distraction of the wayfarer. In the first case the swift-moving hansom or gig would fling sheets of such soup—where not intercepted by trousers or skirts—completely across the pavement, so that the frontages of the Strand throughout its length had an eighteen-inch plinth of mud-parge thus imposed upon it. The pea-soup conditions was met by wheeled "mud-carts" each attended by two ladlers clothed as for Icelandic seas in thigh boots, oilskins collared to the chin, and sou'westers sealing in the back

55

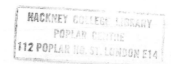

of the neck. Splash Ho! The foot passenger now gets the mud in his eye! The axle-grease condition was met by horse-mechanized brushes and travellers in the small hours found fire-hoses washing away residues . . .

And after the mud the noise, which, again endowed by the horse, surged like a mighty heart-beat in the central districts of London's life. It was a thing beyond all imaginings. The streets of workaday London were uniformly paved in "granite" sets . . . and the hammering of a multitude of iron-shod hairy heels upon [them], the deafening, side-drum tattoo of tyred wheels jarring from the apex of one set to the next like sticks dragging along a fence; the creaking and groaning and chirping and rattling of vehicles, light and heavy, thus maltreated; the jangling of chain harness and the clanging or jingling of every other conceivable thing else, augmented by the shrieking and bellowings called for from those of God's creatures who desired to impart information or proffer a request vocally—raised a din that . . . is beyond conception. It was not any such paltry thing as noise. It was an immensity of sound . . .

from an article describing the London of 1890 by H. B. Cresswell
in *Architectural Review* (December 1958)

London Bridge, c. 1870

London Pleasures—by Gaslight

Mother took us to the Wild West show and we crowded on stages like football field stands and watched a gory drama played out on the turf below, and had an experience like that which Hiram Percy Maxim records about himself in that American classic of family humour and eccentricity, *A Genius in the Family*. Hiram P. Maxim tells how as a boy he was taken to an Indian play at the theatre. He had never been to the theatre before and took Indians very seriously. In fact he disliked them. So when the people on the stage began to worry about the coming of the Indians, he began to worry too. He suggested to his mother that they might escape while the going was good. Out in the street there would be a policeman handy to protect them. With great obstinacy his mother refused to budge but that did not console him at all and when the Indians actually bounded, whooping, on to the stage he made one leap for the aisle and started for the street shouting at the very top of his lungs, "Come on, Mamma!"

And Mamma came.

Now nothing quite as bad as that happened to me. But there down below me was a Wild West homestead and a cattle corral and it was Mother who told me, in reply to my persistent inquiries, that Indians would be coming presently. I had been reading an Indian serial in *The Scout* and like Maxim had formed a poor opinion of them which Fenimore Cooper had not yet had the chance to correct. If they were real Indians would it not be dangerous to stay here? Didn't Mother think that we ought to go and ought not one to warn the people down there who were not protected by fences or anything?

"They're only pretending, you fool," said my brother with scorn.

Well, that was all right, I maintained, so long as they kept pretending. But would they? They were real Indians and with tomahawks and rifles and ponies the temptation would be just to be real Indians rather than pretend to be Indians only pretending. I doubted their good faith. After all, many a bigger boy had said he was "just pretending" only to give you the mother of all whacks or to play you the kind of trick which showed that human nature was not to be trusted after all.

E

57

"Shut up, you baby," said Kenneth.

"I won't bring you again," said Mother.

Presently the pleasant Wild West scene of milking a cow and rounding up cattle, drawing water from a well or coddling the baby on the porch was transformed. Someone came riding in like mad, pointing and yelling "Indians!" and everyone ran around, just as they did in Hiram P. Maxim's play, screaming, which was upsetting. Even my sophisticated brother began to look worried and Mother, who always implicitly believed in the reality of any play she saw, began to exclaim in concern. So when I asked "Well why don't they run away, Mummy? They could run over here," she nodded, tight-lipped, in vigorous agreement. "The stupids. The stupids," she said. "I wouldn't wait if there were Indians around."

"I'd run!"

"Shush," Kenneth said.

Shushing was no use. The Indians poured into the arena riding their fast, athletic, showy ponies. They whooped and yelled and fired their guns into the air and made their horses rear and were covered with feathers and grease paint and looked as terrifying as a legion of devils. The white people at the ranch thought so too. The men fired at the Indians, but the women screamed and screamed. And the Indians rode around and around in a streaming circle firing guns and arrows and presently they fired fire arrows and one of them ran up and set alight to a house *with people inside* and was shot as he got away.

Mother was bobbing up and down in an agony and so was I, but I was most concerned with my own skin and pulled at her elbow. I said I didn't believe they were only pretending, and I could see that my brother had doubts too, and when the woman with the baby ran out of the burning house and an Indian rode her down and scalped her my brother clenched his fists and his teeth and jumped up ready to run down and fight them himself.

"The cads!" he said, "fighting against women and children. The dirty rotters."

from *The Living Hedge* by Leslie Pau

SPRING-HEEL'D JACK:

THE TERROR OF LONDON.

THE FATE OF GRASPER.

"The Fate of Grasper" from a Penny Dreadful

Next door to the Whitechapel Police Station, in Leman Street, is th
Garrick Theatre. Gallery, one penny; pit, twopence; boxes, three
pence. The pieces played at this establishment are, of course
adapted to the audience—the aristocrats among whom pay three
pence for their seats. The first time we penetrated its gloom
passages, great excitement prevailed. The company were performin
the "Starving Poor of Whitechapel"; and at the moment of our entr
the stage policemen were getting very much the worst of a fre
fight, to the unbounded delight of pit and gallery. The sympathie
of the audience, however, were kindly. They leant to the starveling
and the victim of fate; for four out of five understood only too we
what hard life in Whitechapel meant: and had spent nights with th
stars, upon the stones of London. In this, and kindred establish
ments, the helper of "a female in distress" (dismissed from the Wes
End long ago) is sure of his rounds of applause. The drama wa
roughly performed. An infant prodigy (whom the manager after
wards introduced to us) piped its lines of high-flown sentimen
intelligently; the manager himself took the leading part in a broad
stagey sort of way, excellently well adapted to the audience—t
judge from their applause; and everything was spiced highly t
touch the tough palates of a Whitechapel audience.

*   *   *   *   *

A recent writer on the season, tells us that balls are on the decline
because only very young men—and, I presume, not very advantag
eous ones, matrimonially considered,—can be got to stand up; an
that therefore "devotion for life, dearest," is now "bad form durin
dance music". A *déjeuner* is recommended as not a bad opportunit
—if the words need be said at all; but a garden party is the lates
thing in opportunities for breaking fresh ground. A garden party is
good—a very good opportunity, and so is Hurlingham: but do eithe
equal a thorough croquet party?

Archery and croquet are two out-door amusements of fashionabl
London which no foreigner understands. They are conducted with
demureness and serious, business-like precision, that look more lik
performances of strict duty, than the *abandon* of pleasure, to th

superficial observer. These are the hours for sentiment. It may be said that a man is nearer the church-door when he has a mallet in his hand, than when to the strains of Godfrey, he has his arm round a lady's waist.

Beyond all doubt the amusement that delights the largest number of the cultivated in London, is the opera. It is the quiet evening of the fagging pleasure week. The opera and then home, is an off-night which is delightful to the weary traveller from garden party, to tea, to dinner, to conversazione, and rout, and ball—who has no rest from sunset to sunrise, and is then due in the park in the morning. Or it is an hour's rest, before the fatigues of the night begin. "As one cannot go to bed in the middle of the afternoon—11.30 p.m.—it is necessary to go somewhere after the opera," is the declaration of a well-known *poseur* on the subject. Without the opera, the pleasures of a London season would count its victims by the score. "That model of a meritorious English gentleman"—as Lucy Aiken described John Evelyn, said—"For my part I profess that I delight in a cheerful gaiety, affect and cultivate variety; the universe itself were not beautiful to me without it." The gaiety which meritorious English gentlemen of our day affect, often ceases to be cheerful; and they discover a deadening sameness in the variety of the round of pleasure which circulates from the meeting of Parliament, till Goodwood. From the weariness of the round, the opera is the glorious and delightful rest. It is repose to the body, and comfort to the mind.

The barrel organ is the opera of the street-folk: and Punch is their national comedy theatre. I cannot call to mind any scene on our many journeys through London that struck the authors of this pilgrimage more forcibly than the waking up of a dull, woe-begone alley, to the sound of an organ. The women leaning out of the windows—pleasurably stirred, for an instant, in that long disease, their life—and the children trooping and dancing round the swarthy player!

It is equalled only by the stir and bustle, and cessation of employment, which happens when the man who carries the greasy old stage of Mr Punch, halts at a favourable "pitch"; and begins to drop the green baize behind which he is to play the oftenest performed serio-comic drama in the world. The milk-woman stops on her rounds: the baker deliberately unshoulders his load: the newsboy (never at a loss for a passage of amusement on his journey) forgets that he is the bearer of the "special edition": the policeman halts on his beat—while the pipes are tuning, and the wooden actors are being made ready within, and dog Toby is staring sadly round upon the mob. We have all confessed to the indefinable witchery of the heartless rogue of the merry eye and ruby nose, whose career—so far as we are permitted to know it—is an unbroken round of facetious brutalities. Wife-beating is second nature to him. To be sure Judy does not look all that man can desire in the partner of his bosom. The dog, indeed, makes the best appearance; and is the most reputable member of this notorious family.

from *London—a Pilgrimage* by Doré and Jerrold

London Pleasures—by Gaslight

Skating, for example, was perhaps first seen in England by Mr Pepys and his contemporaries on the ice of the canal in St James's; and a century later fashionable London flocked to admire the agility of Lord Carlisle and Mr Benjamin West, the painter, on the Serpentine, when my Lord March came up in a carriage wrapped in three bearskins, with his hands in a muff, and his carriage warmed with a portable stove, and watched a company of his friends walking through a minuet on the ice. There was much primitive cricket too in Hyde Park in the reign of George the Second, when the citizen could watch Frederick Prince of Wales and a dozen of men of birth and great station at the humble exercises of the game in its earlier and undeveloped periods. Improvised prize-rings were another attraction of the second half of the eighteenth century, when Ben Green of Carnaby Market would fight "Chitty" Myers of the Adelphi on a Sunday morning, and provide so popular an entertainment that thirty sportsmen who were watching the fun on one limb of an elm came to the ground by the breaking of the branch, and half of them were conveyed to Chelsea Hospital. Finally, although no one ever perhaps fought a duel for pleasure, the chance of seeing an encounter was a distinct addition to the joys of Hyde Park for certain minds, and from the days of Hamilton and Mohun to those of Fox and Adair, the mere rumour of such an encounter would bring such crowds as would often prevent the meeting taking place at all.

We all know the part which the parks fill in the lives of Londoners today, or if we sometimes forget it, it may be easily realized by imagining for a moment Hyde Park and St James's, the Green Park and Regent's Park, to say nothing of Battersea Park, Victoria Park, and Finsbury Park, and others farther afield, cut up and devoted to streets of smug villas or workmen's dwellings. The pleasures which we have recalled have been exchanged for others which are shared by thousands of humbler people, and the parks themselves have surely changed for the better in every respect but that of a quaint rusticity since Sir Robert Walpole hunted the otter in St James's. There are even compensations for the Londoner in that same connection of the *rus in urbe;* the intelligent manipulation of shrub and flower border, with their masses of lovely colour, which greets one in most of our great parks is surely a model for all operations of the sort; and there are certainly worse places in which to study the amusing idiosyncrasies of many wild creatures, ringdoves say, or water-hens or seagulls, than the little garden at the foot of the Serpentine, or the Long Water in St James's Park.

from *Amusements of Old London* by W. J. Boulton

Under the trees, Regent's Park

Bank holidays were much the same for Londoners as they are now—a day for remaining at home or for getting as far away as possible. In this matter we divided. Mother and I did the one, and my father and the boys the other. They used to start off by an early train, and take one of their colossal walks into the country, or else go fishing in the River Lea. Then off went the servants somewhere (probably to Hampstead Heath) for the entire day. Mother and I stayed at home to enjoy what she called "the freedom of the wild ass", with no lessons, no proper meals, no duty walks, and above all no chance of callers. As soon as the boys had gone I used to watch for the big waggonettes full of children going off to Chingford or Epping for the day. They used to sing and wave flags, and I waved to them. After this the neighbourhood became sepulchral—"silence like a poultice came to heal the blows of sound". Mother must have been very clever in thinking up jolly things to do, for I can never remember feeling dull or out of it when the boys went off anywhere. She had the knack of vicarious enjoyment, and we used to live through what the others were probably doing: "Now they are having their sand-wiches", "Now I expect they have caught some fish", "Perhaps Charles has done a sketch".

After tea it was my cue to watch at the window for the return of the wagonettes. I must say I took a grim pleasure in the peevish tones that came from the tired children, and the scoldings of the mothers, not to mention their lack of song and flag-waving. Our next business was to lay the cloth for supper and make a big spread for the hungry home-comers. At one such evening meal mother exclaimed, "How well you look, Dym!" The others smiled in a gratified way and spoke of the health-giving properties of country walking. It was not till many days had passed that they told her how Dym had fallen into the river and barely been saved from drowning. He had been taken to an inn, put into a hot bath, rubbed down, wrapped in blankets while his clothes were dried, and given whisky. No wonder, as he was hurried home as fast as possible, that he looked a bit rosy. He had a delicate chest, and had once been at death's door, while we crept about the house, alarmed at the arrival of a second doctor.

Strange as it seems today, when excursions are so cheap, a London family often went without any "summer holiday" at all. There were certainly "excursion trains", but they meant all that was horrible: long and unearthly hours, packed carriages, queer company, continual shuntings aside and waiting for regular trains to go by, and worst of all the contempt of decent travellers. We had a little rhyme about them which ended:

> *Grown old and rusted, the boiler busted*
> *And smashed the excursion train.*

So for a large family a trip to the sea-side was an expensive affair.

from *A London Child of the Seventies* by M. Vivian Hughes

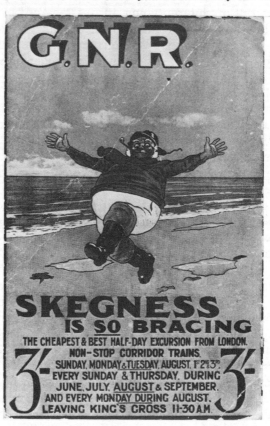

London at War
1914–1918

It was appropriate that two so interested in the After Life as Auntie Florrie and I should be together on the night the world ended. It happened one Friday in the war while mother was shopping at the Co-op. Auntie Florrie was upstairs in the lavatory, Grandma was having a bath, and I had just begun to write my first story in a penny exercise book. It was to be a full length story and illustrated by the author, whose portrait I was drawing when my penny ink bottle rose gracefully in the best poltergeist tradition and emptied itself over my book. Beyond the drawn blind and visible through it despite the gaslight, shone a vast and awful sheet of flame. A tremendous explosion shook the house and made the ground tremble. The tinkling of glass in the silence which followed sounded pleasant, like the clash of the tinklers hung in the hall which made music now, as they did when the wind caught them, or Kenneth and I ran through the hall and bashed them.

"Zeppelins, Auntie," I shouted, rushing into the passage. "Zeppelins, Grandma! Are you all right?"

"Gee whizz," Auntie shouted down. "I'm all right. Seems to me like the end of the world's come."

A gust of the supernatural hit me and I shouted up again. "Come on down, Auntie. Come on down, Grandma, and don't talk silly. Mother wouldn't go out shopping if it was."

"I'm coming as quick as I can," Auntie answered. "You stay right where you are and don't go near the door in case there's anything more."

"If it's the end of the world they don't need anything more," I shouted, always most angry when I was most frightened. "What on earth are you doing up there?"

For answer there was another alarming crash as Grandma, trying to get dried and dressed quickly, fell on the bathroom floor. She thought this was a Zeppelin attack on her personally and cried out for Aunt Florrie.

"Lairdsakes," said Aunt Florrie darting to her aid. Without waiting for them any more I opened the front door, for the street was full of the sound of rushing feet.

The whole world at the street end was aflame. A great sheet of fire hung in the sky, lighting up frightened faces of the people running towards it. I was filled with panic at the sight of them; there was something eerie in their absorbed surge towards catastrophe. Thus people might run to take refuge in God if the end had come.

"What's up? What is it?" I screamed at them.

They did not wait to talk. They pointed to the flame which stood like judgment in the sky.

"Wells'!" they shouted. "Wells'!"

Wells' was an explosive factory just across the railway line. It consisted of a lot of tin sheds dotted along the edge of a golf course. It can't be Wells', I thought, it's much too big.

My aunt joined me, holding me firmly by the collar as though I were a dog that might bolt.

Grandma, still shaken and complaining, followed her, clutching the door in case another one went off.

"They say it's Wells'. I don't believe it," I shouted.

"Just look at that," my aunt said calmly, joining the people who were staring rapt at the beautiful and immense aurora over heaven. "It may be Wells', but personally, honey, I'd say a prayer right away. I wouldn't put it beyond God to put an end to this wicked world at any time."

My aunt's calm consideration of the matter was as infuriating as it was frightening. God just would not let the world end while Mother and Marjorie were at the Co-op. All the same, if you thought of the earth as being flat as a biscuit then it looked indeed as though one edge had caught fire and before long we should burn too. If, on the other hand, you thought of it as a ball which was on fire in the middle, then the flames which had burst through the crust not very far away might at any moment run through the garden path under my feet. I saw both possibilities with terrifying clearness and lifted my feet alternately, gingerly and surreptitiously feeling them to see if they were hot.

"Mother!" I said to Auntie, thinking suddenly that Mother might be in it. "And Kenneth?"

"God will look after them," Auntie said.

"Not if He's ending the world," I said.

Mrs Barratt who lived down the road and whose son Bertie went to school with me, collapsed moaning at our gate. Aunt supported her while I went for a chair and a glass of water.

"My son Teddy, my son Teddy," she lamented when she came to. "He's at Wells' tonight."

"God will watch over him," said Auntie, rosy with confidence. "Just pray."

"My poor Teddy, I'm sure he's gone," the old lady wept. "I know I'll never see him again."

I knew Teddy, and had played cricket with him, and I wept too, but I was sure Mrs Barratt was unreasonable in being so certain that he was dead.

"It isn't Wells'. I'll bet it's Woolwich Arsenal," I said. "He must be all right. I'll see," and though my aunt shouted to me to stop I ran out of the gate and joined the stragglers after the main mob which had gone towards Wells'. When I reached the station it was plain that Wells' was unhurt. The railway banks were dark and quiet, and the peaceful, wooded One Tree Hill beyond with its square church tower was redly lit by the fire from the east.

When I told Mrs Barratt, she said, "D'you think my Teddy's all right?" "Of course," I said angrily, but as I took her arm and helped her across to her home she kept murmuring broken-heartedly, ignoring all my assurances, "My poor Teddy, my poor little Teddy."

As there seemed to be no immediate likelihood of a repetition of the disaster, Auntie Florrie gave me permission to run down to the main street to meet Mother. I ran through streets crowded with people watching the eastern light and assuring each other that it was Woolwich Arsenal with the certainty that a short while ago they had been saying it was Wells'. I passed a gesticulating old gentleman with a prophetic white beard and silver hair bearing a paper banner inscribed "Repent, for the Kingdom of God is at hand".

"The end of the world has come!" he was shouting and the crowds went hushed and respectful as he passed. "It's the end of the world," he cried. "Repent! Repent!" We all thought suddenly of our unforgiven sins.

I fell happily and excitedly on my mother, brother, and sister when I found them. God had spared them after all: God had looked after us.

"*Well*," said my mother as she stood in the kitchen unpinning her hat. Her eyes were shining with excitement. "Well..." She searched with all the drama of her nature for the most telling and appropriate words.

"What happened in the Co-op, Mum? Tell us," I urged.

What had happened was dramatic enough. The lights had gone out and the women went hysterical but Mother climbed on to the counter and shouted to them to behave and ordered the manageress to light some candles. Mother was not ready to tell this yet. She searched for an overture to the drama.

"Well! The lights went out and the whole sky was filled with one sheet of flame and I had the funniest feeling. 'Lottie,' I said to myself, 'it's the end of the world.'"

Black headlines in the morning paper told us that the munition works at Silvertown had blown up and Monty Law, who sat next to me at school boasted that all his windows were blown in. "Over my bed, too," he said eagerly, "and me in it." "Coo," said a neighbour, "d'you go to bed as early as that? What d'you think, men, old Lawy goes to bed at seven with the kids."

Everyone jeered at Monty who blushed deeply and bit his lips and did not know what to say.

"I never go to bed before ten," I lied, anxious always to be in the right swim. "At least, hardly ever."

from The Living Hedge by Leslie Paul

Days Drawing In

The days fail: night broods over afternoon:
And at my child's first drink beyond the night
Her skin is silver in the early light.
Sweet the grey morning and the raiders gone.

E. J. Scovell

1939-1945

These were the times when the English, and particularly the Londoners, who had the place of honour, were seen at their best. Grim and gay, dogged and serviceable, with the confidence of an unconquered people in their bones, they adapted themselves to this strange new life, with all its terrors, with all its jolts and jars. One evening when I was leaving for an inspection on the East Coast, on my way to King's Cross the sirens sounded, the streets began to empty, except for long queues of very tired, pale people, waiting for the last bus that would run. An autumn mist and drizzle shrouded the scene. The air was cold and raw. Night and the enemy were approaching. I felt, with a spasm of mental pain, a deep sense of the strain and suffering that was being borne throughout the world's largest capital city. How long would it go on? How much more would they have to bear? What were the limits of their vitality? What effects would their exhaustion have upon our productive war-making power?. . . .

Under the pressure of the bombardment the shelters and defences grew continually. I was worried principally on three accounts. The first was the drains. When you had six or seven million people living in a great built-up area the smashing of their sewers and water supply seemed to me a very great danger. Could we keep the sewage system working or would there be a pestilence? What would happen if the drains got into the water supply? Actually, early in October the main sewage outfall was destroyed and we had to let all our sewage flow into the Thames, which stank, first of sewage, and afterwards of the floods of chemicals we poured into it. But all was mastered. Secondly, I feared that the long nights for millions in the crowded street shelters—only blast-proof at that—would produce epidemics of influenza, diphtheria, the common cold and what not. But it appeared that Nature had already provided against this danger. Man is a gregarious animal, and apparently the mischievous microbes he inhales fight and neutralize each other. They go out and devour each other, and Man walks off unharmed. If this is not scientifically correct, then it ought to be. The fact remains that during this rough winter the health of the Londoners was actually above the average. Moreover, the power of enduring suffering in the ordinary people of every country, when their spirit is roused, seemed to have no bounds.

My third fear was a glass famine. Sometimes whole streets had every window-frame smashed by the blast of a single bomb. . . . I was however reassured by facts and figures and this danger also never came to pass. . . .

These pages certainly cannot attempt to describe the problems of London government, when often night after night ten or twenty thousand people were made homeless, and when nothing but the ceaseless vigil of the citizens as Fire Guards on the roofs prevented uncontrollable conflagrations; when hospitals, filled with mutilated men and women, were themselves struck by the enemy's bombs; when hundreds of thousands of weary people crowded together in unsafe and insanitary shelters; when communications by road and rail were ceaselessly broken down; when drains were smashed and light, power and gas paralysed; and when nevertheless the whole fighting, toiling life of London had to go forward, and nearly a million people be moved in and out for their work every night and morning. . . .

from *The Second World War: Volume II—Their Finest Hour*
by Winston S. Churchill

London, 1944

The Wall

It was our third job that night.

Until this thing happened, work had been without incident. There had been shrapnel, a few inquiring bombs, and some huge fires; but these were unremarkable and have since merged without identity into the neutral maze of fire and noise and water and night, without date and without hour, with neither time nor form, that lowers mistily at the back of my mind as a picture of the air-raid season.

I suppose we were worn down and shivering. Three a.m. is a mean-spirited hour. I suppose we were drenched, with the cold hose-water trickling in at our collars and settling down at the tails of our shirts. Without doubt the heavy brass couplings felt moulded from metal-ice. Probably the open roar of the pumps drowned the petulant buzz of the raiders above, and certainly the ubiquitous fire-glow made an orange stage-set of the streets. Black water would have puddled the City alleys and I suppose our hands and our faces were black as the water. Black with hacking about among the burnt-up rafters. These things were an every-night nonentity. They happened and they were not forgotten because they were never even remembered.

But I do remember it was our third job. And there we were—Len, Lofty, Verno and myself, playing a fifty-foot jet up the face of a tall city warehouse and thinking of nothing at all. You don't think of anything after the first few hours. You just watch the white pole of water lose itself in the fire and you think of nothing. Sometimes you move the jet over to another window. Sometimes the orange dims to black but you only ease your grip on the ice-cold nozzle and continue pouring careless gallons through the window. You know the fire will fester for hours yet. However, that night the blank indefinite hours of waiting were sharply interrupted—by an unusual sound. Very suddenly a long rattling crack of bursting brick and mortar perforated the moment. And then the upper half of that five-storey building heaved over towards us. It hung there, poised for a timeless second before rumbling down at us. I was thinking of nothing at all and then I was thinking of everything in the world.

In that simple second my brain digested every detail of the scene. New eyes opened at the sides of my head so that, from within, I photographed a hemispherical panorama bounded by the huge length of the building in front of me and the narrow lane on either side.

Blocking us on the left was the squat trailer pump, roaring and quivering with effort. Water throbbed from its overflow valves and from leakages in the hose and couplings. A ceaseless stream spewed down its grey sides into the gutter. But nevertheless a fat iron exhaust-pipe glowed red-hot in the middle of the wet engine. I had to look past Lofty's face. Lofty was staring at the controls, hands tucked into his armpits for warmth. Lofty was thinking of nothing. He had a black diamond of soot over one eye, like the White-Eyed Kaffir in negative.

To the other side of me was a free run up the alley. Overhead swung a sign—"Catto and Henley". I wondered what in hell they sold. Old Stamps ? . . . The alley was quite free.

Behind me, Len and Verno shared the weight of the hose. They heaved up against the strong backward drag of the water pressure. All I had to do was yell "Drop it"—and then run. We could risk the live hose snaking up at us. We could run to the right down the free alley—Len, Verno and me. But I never moved. I never said "Drop it" or anything else. That long second held me hypnotized, rubber boots cemented to the pavement. Ton upon ton of red-hot brick hovering in the air above us numbed all initiative. I could only think. I couldn't move.

Six yards in front stood the blazing building. A minute before I would never have distinguished it from any other drab Victorian atrocity happily on fire. Now I was immediately certain of every minute detail. The building was five storeys high. The top four storeys were fiercely alight. The rooms inside were alive with red fire. The black outside walls remained untouched. And thus, like the lighted carriages of a night express, there appeared alternating rectangles of black and red that emphasized vividly the extreme symmetry of the window spacing: each oblong window-shape posed a vermilion panel set in perfect order upon the dark face of the wall. There were ten windows to each floor, making forty windows in all. In rigid rows of ten, one row placed precisely above the other, with strong contrasts of black and red, the blazing windows stood to attention in strict formation. The oblong building, the oblong windows, the oblong spacing. Orange-red colour seemed to *bulge*

Fires in London's dockland after heavy air-raids

from the black frame-work, assumed tactile values, like boiling jelly that expanded inside a thick black squared grill.

Three of the storeys, thirty blazing windows and their huge frame of black brick, a hundred solid tons of hard, deep Victorian wall, pivoted over towards us and hung flatly over the alley. Whether the descending wall actually paused in its fall I can never know. Probably it never did. Probably it only seemed to hang there. Probably my eyes only digested its action at an early period of momentum, so that I saw it "off true" but before it had gathered speed.

The night grew darker as the great mass hung over us. Through smoke-fogged fireglow the moonlight had hitherto penetrated to the pit of our alley through declivities in the skyline. Now some of the moonlight was being shut out as the wall hung ever further over us. The wall shaded the moonlight like an inverted awning. Now the pathway of light above had been squeezed to a thin line. That was the only silver lining I ever believed in. It shone out—a ray of hope. But it was declining hope, for although at this time the entire hemispherical scene appeared static, an imminence of movement could be sensed throughout—presumably because the scene was actually moving. Even the speed of the shutter which closed the photograph on my mind was powerless to exclude this motion from a deeper consciousness. The picture appeared static to the limited surface sense, the eyes and the material brain, but beyond that there was hidden movement.

The second was timeless. I had leisure to remark many things. For instance, that an iron derrick, slightly to the left, would not hit me. The derrick stuck out from the building and I could feel its sharpness and hardness as clearly as if I had run my body intimately over its contour. I had time to notice that it carried a foot-long hook, a chain with three-inch rings, two girder supports and a wheel more than twice as large as my head.

A wall will fall in many ways. It may sway over to one side or the other. It may crumble at the very beginning of its fall. It may remain intact and fall flat. This wall fell as flat as a pancake. It clung to its shape through ninety degrees to the horizontal. Then it detached itself from the pivot and slammed down on top of us.

The last resistance of bricks and mortar at the pivot point cracked off like automatic gun fire. The violent sound both deafened us and brought us to our senses. We dropped the hose and crouched. Afterwards Verno said that I knelt slowly on one knee with bowed head, like a man about to be knighted. Well, I got my knighting. There was an incredible noise—a thunderclap condensed into the space of an eardrum—and then the bricks and the mortar came tearing and burning into the flesh of my face.

Lofty, away by the pump, was killed. Len, Verno and myself they dug out. There was very little brick on top of us. We had been lucky. We had been framed by one of those symmetrical, oblong window spaces.

from *The Wall* by William Sansom

East End Redeveloped

The general attitude was summed up by Mr Jeffreys.

"I've got plenty of friends around here. I've always got on well with people, but I don't invite anyone here. I've got friends at work and friends at sport and friends I have a drink with. I know all the people around here, and I'm not invited into anyone else's home either. It doesn't seem right somehow. Your home's your own."

Where every front door opens on to street or staircase, and houses are crowded on top of one another, such an attitude helps to preserve some privacy against the press of people.

This exclusiveness in the home runs alongside an attitude of friendliness to other people living in the same street. Quite often people have themselves lived there for a long time—one out of every ten women and one out of every twenty men in the general sample still live in the street where they were born—and consequently know many of the older residents well. Quite often, too, either they or their neighbours also have relatives in the street who add to the spread of social contacts. If a person gets on bad terms with another person in the street—like Mrs Shipway whose neighbour "started spreading stories about me and told me off for sending my children to Mum's when I go out to work"—she is also on bad terms with her family. "They're all related in this street," said Mr Lamb. "It's awful, you can't talk to anyone in the street about any of the others, but you find it's a relation. You have to be very careful." But if he is careful and keeps on good terms with his neighbours, he is also on good terms with their relatives, and can nod to them in the street, knowing that he will get a response. He only has to stand at his front door to find someone out of his past who is also in his present.

"I suppose people who come here from outside think it's an awful place, but us established ones like it. Here you can just open the door and say hello to everybody."

The streets are known as "turnings", and adjoining ones as "backdoubles". Surrounded by their human associations, the words had a glow to them. "In our turning *we*", they would say, "do this, that, or the other." "I've lived in this turning for fifty years", said one old man proudly, "and here I intend to stay." The residents of the turning who usually make up a sort of "village" of 100 to 200 people, have their own places to meet, where few outsiders ever come—practically every turning has its one or two pubs, its two or three shops, and its "bookie's runner". They organize their own parties: nearly every turning had its committee and celebration (and several built wooden stages for the display of local talent) for the Coronation of 1953. Some turnings have little war memorials built on to walls of houses with inscriptions like the following:

R. I. P.
IN LOVING MEMORY OF THE MEN OF CYPRUS STREET
WHO MADE THE GREAT SACRIFICE
1914–1918
J. AMOS, E. AGOMBAR, A. BOARDMAN, A. H. COLE . . .

—there follow the names of the other twenty-two soldiers from Cyprus Street. Above it is a smaller plaque to the men killed in 1939–45: "They are marching with their comrades somewhere on the road ahead." Pots and vases of flowers are fixed in a half circle to the wall; they are renewed regularly by the women of the turning, who make a street collection every Armistice Day.

There is the same kind of feeling in the few small courts still standing where a few houses face each other across a common front-yard. In one of these, the houses are covered from top to bottom with green trellis-work, tiers of window boxes stand out from the trellis, and on one wall is a proliferation of flowers around a war memorial, a Union Jack, and some faded pictures of the Queen. One of the residents told us, with evident satisfaction, that she was born in the same courtyard house that she had lived in for sixty-two years and spoke with slight disparagement of her neighbours: "They're new here—they've only been here eighteen years." She had been shocked to hear that the authorities might be labelling her beloved court a "slum", and was now terrified lest they pull it down.

from *Family and Kinship in East London* by Young and Willmott

But it was no good. In spite of "Ivan's" efforts with petitions and the placards outside her house saying: *Leave us alone—We have done no wrong*; in spite of her marching up and down the Old Kent Road shouting "Judgment Day is Upon Us", the Council won. Soon the removal vans came to fill up and tip out as families left to move into new blocks of flats.

Mrs Bloggs was the first to go. They said that the bed was moved with her husband still sleeping in it, and that she ordered the men not to bump too much because he must get his eight hours. Nobody saw Old Ginger Nut and her dogs go, but one morning the men came to board up her windows with red, yellow and green doors. Some said she had moved during the night so that we couldn't see her rubbish; others said she was still in there, rotting away with her husbands, and it wasn't worth troubling her, she wouldn't notice if the house was pulled down on top of her.

Soon the street was silent and empty, festering in the heat like a cat lying dead in the gutter. Occasionally you heard a hammering as another street door was barred forever or you heard the swearing of a tramp being turned out of his new home.

from *London Morning* by Valerie Avery

East End Slum, 1912

In their place rises the new Bethnal Green, whose symbol is the soaring glass and concrete of the Council flats. More rebuilding has been done locally than in other parts of London: "A third of all the slum clearance work done by the London County Council since 1945 has taken place in the East End, although this area forms only 6.5 per cent of the County." The effects are apparent. In 1957 we found that Council property accounted for less than a third of the dwellings in Bethnal Green; by 1964 the proportion was more than a half. The flats are in many styles—point block, slab or cluster block; some massive and ponderous; others delicate and light on podium supports; elsewhere cliffs of glass and curtain-walling dwarf the low promontories of the four-storey maisonettes. As well as the skyline—still dealing out surprises as one turns an unfamiliar corner or glances over the roofs from the top of a bus in Bethnal Green Road—there is a new variety at ground level. There is, for instance, the paved Market Square off Roman Road where, surrounded by new shops, new flats and a new pub (The Weaver's Arms), the stall-holders from Roman Road itself now do a noisy trade. On one housing scheme there is the familiar carpet of railed-off turf between the tall blocks; on another, cobbled foregrounds; on a third, a small hillock, furnished with white fencing and topped by a sculptured mother and child who would barely disgrace the near-by Whitechapel Art Gallery.

The new shops deserve special notice, because they illustrate how Bethnal Green is becoming part of the wider society. Until a few years ago the place never had a Woolworths; now it has a brightly lit new one. The giant new supermarket, a few yards away, offers a range of foods previously unknown to most local housewives— Camembert, mortadello, chop suey, pâté de foie gras. The East End, though not so much Bethnal Green in particular, has always catered for the tastes of its immigrant minorities, but this is something different: it represents an extension of local horizons and of freedom of choice.

The insides of people's homes have changed as well. More households have a separate home of their own:

Bryan Wills, aged 15, lived with his parents and younger sister in a three-bedroomed flat in a new Council block.

To reach the flat means travelling up six storeys in the aluminium lift that stops at alternate floors—at the other end of the tiled entrance hall is the lift for floors three, five and seven. (As a result, Bryan's family does not know the people immediately above or below.) A ring at the illuminated bell-push labelled "Mr and Mrs J. B. Wills" and into the thickly carpeted hall. The kitchen had an electric cooker with eye-level grill, a white enamelled sink unit, a tall refrigerator, a red formica-topped table and four stools upholstered in red and black plastic. The interview took place in the living-room, which had a wide view over the chimney-pots and the tiny work-shops in the foreground to more tall blocks and beyond to the River Thames. The room was large and dustless, with an enamel and chrome electric heater filling the fireplace. Loose covers in a broad autumn-leaf print were smoothed carefully over the chairs and sofa, and various ornaments—a miniature ship's wheel enclosing a a thermometer, a cruet set labelled "A Present from Herne Bay", a felt scotch terrier dressed in a tartan kilt—were arranged in a straight line along the mantelpiece. A framed studio photograph of Bryan, taken about three years earlier, stood beneath a table lamp on the television set.

from *Adolescent Boys of East London* by Peter Willmott

Working from this plan, even before the war ended, London took powers under a wartime act to combat "blitz and blight", to designate a huge area within a modern borough of Tower Hamlets as an area of comprehensive redevelopment, which meant that all reconstruction would be carried through according to a master plan prepared by the planning authority. By 1960 this area of nearly two square miles was still the biggest area of comprehensive development in Britain. The plan involved nothing less than the creation of a new town within the heavily built-up area of inner London, to hold close on 100,000 people—compared with over 100,000 in 1951 and over 200,000 in 1939. It is expected to be virtually finished by the late 1970s, and it has already been joined by two other schemes on the northern flank which will increase the total area under comprehensive reconstruction by nearly one-fifth as much again. The result on the ground, in the mid-1960s, is dramatic. Huge areas are in a state of travail. Bulldozers, cranes, steel frames and builders' fences dominate whole tracts of the East End. In other places are already finished neighbourhoods: here is a totally new world, dominated by the tall blocks of flats and by the lower terraces of three- and four-storey maisonettes, standing in spacious gardens and landscaped squares. Only a few yards away stand the reminders of the past: the long, squat rows of cottages inhabited by dock labourers or Jewish tailors. But they invariably already have the air of waiting for the demolition men.

from World Cities by Peter Hall

The New East-Enders

And this is the terminus of truths?
Objective of the dreams and all
The speculations we saved up
A lifetime and paid for—
This dust and this laterite?

And this the welcome that awaits us?
The glossy pamphlets promised
During the long hours to console
A tedious journey,
This dust on a barren ground?

Are we really arrived, have we
Really reached, as the smooth guide says,
The great and beautiful city—
Where the perennials open and thornless
Branch upon branch enrich the sky?

Dust grits my eye.

"Arrival" by Ee Tiang Hong

The Lament of the Banana Man

Gal, I'm tellin' you, I'm tired fo' true
Tired of Englan', tired o' you.
But I can't go back to Jamaica now . . .

I'm here in Englan', I'm drawin pay,
I go to de underground every day—
Eight hours is all, half-hour fo' lunch,
M' uniform's free, an' m' ticket punch—
Punchin' tickets not hard to do,
When I'm tired o' punchin', I let dem through.

I get a paid holiday once a year.
Ol' age an' sickness can't touch me here.
I have a room of m' own, an' a iron bed,
Dunlopillo under m' head,
A Morphy-Richards to warm de air,
A formica table, an easy chair.
I have summer clothes, an' winter clothes,
An' paper kerchiefs to blow m' nose.

My yoke is easy, my burden is light,
I know a place I can go to, any night.
Dis place Englan'! I'm not complainin',
If it col', it col', if it rainin', it rainin'.
I don't min' if it's mostly night,
Dere's always inside, or de sodium light.
I don't min' white people starin' at me,
Dey don' want me here? Don't is deir country?
You won' catch me bawlin' any homesick tears,
If I don' see Jamaica for a t'ousan' years!

. . . Gal, I'm tellin' you, I'm tired fo' true,
Tired of Englan', tired o' you,
I can't go back to Jamaica now—
But I'd want to die there, anyhow.

                                        Evan Jones

Move to the Suburbs

In some ways the more self-contained home is less self-contained than ever. Greenleigh is part of a larger world. A person's shops are a mile off, his work six miles away, and his relatives ten or twenty miles away, some of them on the suburban circuit of housing estates—Oxhey, Debden, Harold Hill, Becontree—along which no buses ply. Distances to shops, work, and relatives are not walking distances any more. They are motoring distances: a car, like a telephone, can overcome geography and organize a more scattered life into a manageable whole. With a car he can, without having to expose himself to the wintry winds which blow over the fields, get to work, to his relatives in Bethnal Green Road, or to his friends who have gone over to Kent. "Now that we've got the car," said Mr Marsh, "we can see the wife's sister at Laindon more often." She was now seen every fortnight instead of every three or four months. Cars are beginning to move from luxury to necessity. "I don't want to win £75,000. I just want to win £500—so that I can get myself a little car. I could get a nice little car for that. You really need a car down here," said Mr Adams. One of the more fortunate, Mr Berry, who had already achieved the two accomplishments of the complete man, discoursed on their necessity.

"There are two things that I think are essential when you live on an estate. One's a telephone, the other's a car. I don't like having to pay my telephone bill, but I think it's worth it. It means my brother can ring me up on the estate any time he wants to. And if you're in any trouble—if there's anything wrong with one of the boys say—I can ring up a doctor if I need one. You don't need a telephone in Bethnal Green, because the doctor's on the doorstep. Practically anywhere you live in Bethnal Green there's a doctor near at hand. And you need a car for travelling about. We're so far away from everywhere out here that it's actually cheaper to run a car than it is to pay fares."

Greenleigh already has many more telephones than Bethnal Green, where you can go down the street to your relatives as quickly as, and more cheaply than, you can phone them; the figures for residential subscribers are eighty-eight per thousand at Greenleigh and only thirteen in Bethnal Green.

Greenleigh, though composed mainly of manual workers like

Bethnal Green, has nearly seven times more telephones per head and, if our informants are any guide, at least one motive is to keep in touch with the kin left behind. "We can't get up to see them very often," said Mrs Adams. "That's really why we had the phone put in here. If you can only hear each other it's something. It does keep you in touch with home." But if telephones can be installed easily enough, garages cannot. They were not a necessity when the architects made the future in County Hall. A garage, now as rare in twentieth-century Greenleigh as an indoor lavatory was in nineteenth-century Bethnal Green, could be as much a motive for migration in the future. Cars, telephones, telegrams, and letters represent not so much a new and higher standard of life as a means of clinging to something of the old. Where you could walk to your enjoyment, you did not need a car. Where you cannot walk, and public transport is inconvenient or too expensive, you need a car.

This understandable urge to acquisition can easily become competitive. People struggle to raise their all-round standards to those of the home, and in the course of doing so, they look for guidance to their neighbours. To begin with, the first-comers have to make their own way. The later arrivals have their model at hand. The neighbours have put up nice curtains. Have we? They have got their garden planted with privet and new grass-seed. Have we? They have a lawn-mower and a Dunkley pram. What have we got? The new arrivals watch the first-comers, and the first-comers watch the new arrivals. All being under the same pressure for material advance, they naturally mark each other's progress. Those who make the most progress are those who have proved their claim to respectability, Greenleigh style.

from *Family and Class in a London Suburb* by Willmott and Young

Young Voices

I'm often up West, either after work or at the weekends. I like it up there—the pubs and the cafés are more lively and you get more of a mixture of people.

Up the West End, it's really an exploration. We watch all the posh people coming out of their clubs, the way they dress up makes you giggle. And you see a bloke running after a cab for one of these posh people, then a posh bloke gets into the cab as if the other one didn't exist. You learn a lot just watching.

from *Adolescent Boys of East London* by Peter Willmott

The night was glorious out there. The air was sweet as a cool bath, the stars were peeping nosily beyond the neons, and the citizens of the Queendom, in their jeans and separates, were floating down the Shaftesbury Avenue canals, like gondolas. Everyone had loot to spend, everyone a bath with verbena salts behind them, and nobody had broken hearts, because they were all ripe for the easy summer evening.

from *Absolute Beginners* by Colin MacInnes

Just before lighting-up time there are, especially in autumn, sunsets of rare beauty: to look west is to find in the sky that delicate texture of pink and grey which adorns the necks of the town's super-abundant pigeons. It is the hour of release for myriads and of plans for the evening's entertainment. The windows of the soaring offices begin to twinkle. Then comes the adroitly contrived floodlighting of the principal buildings, best seen along the river. It is a fascinating panorama with the contrast of the dark water and the brilliance overhead.

from *The Shell Guide to England—London* by Ivor Brown

Postscript

Whoever thought up the Thames embankment was a genius. It lies curled firm and gentle round the river like a boy does with a girl, after it's over, and it stretches in a great curve from the parliament thing, down there in Westminster, all the way north and east into the City. Going in that way, down-stream, eastwards, it's not so splendid, but when you come back up along it—oh! If the tide's in, the river's like the ocean, and you look across the great wide bend and see the fairy advertising palaces on the south side beaming in the water, and that great white bridge that floats across it gracefully, like a string of leaves. If you're fortunate, the cab gets all the greens, and keeps up the same steady speed, and looking out from the upholstery it's like your own private Cinerama, except that in this one the show's never, never twice the same. And weather makes no difference, or season, it's always wonderful—the magic always works. And just above the diesel whining of the taxi, you hear those *river* noises no one can describe, but you can always recognize. Each time I come here for the ride, in any mood, I get a lift, a rise, a hoist up into joy. And as I gazed out on the water like a mouth, a bed, a sister, I thought how, my God, I love this city, horrible thought it may be, and never ever want to leave it, come what it may send me. Because though it seems so untidy, and so casual, and so keep-your-distance-from-me, if you can get to know this city well enough to twist it round your finger, and if you're its son, it's always on your side, supporting you—or that's what I imagined.

from *Absolute Beginners* by Colin MacInnes

Immigrant Voice

I laughed now out loud at Laddy Boy. "No one will kill me, country-man!" I cried. "This is my city, look at it now!"

from *City of Spades* by Colin MacInnes

87

Further Source Material

Films on London

The Bank of England at Work   Rank 1967   (35 mins)
Barbican   Sound Services 1969   (24 mins)
Fires Were Started (*I Was a Fireman*)   British Film Institute 1943 (80 mins*)
Listen to Britain   British Film Institute 1942   (20 mins*)
The Most Crowded Corner   Central Film Library 1969   (18 mins)
Terminus (early Schlesinger film about Waterloo Station)   British Transport Films 1959   (33 mins*)
We Are the Lambeth Boys   British Film Institute 1959   (52 mins*)
The Living City   Corporation of London Sound Services 1968 (25 mins)

Museums

There are a number of London Museums which are particularly helpful in giving a picture of how ordinary Londoners lived:

Bethnal Green, Museum Ho., Cambridge Heath Road, E2 (*especially toys and costumes*)
Cuming Museum, Walworth Road, Southwark, SE17 (*local; London superstitions*)
Geffrye Museum, Kingsland Road, Shoreditch, E2 (*middle class English home from 1600*)
Hogarth's House, Hogarth Lane, Chiswick, W4
Lancaster House, Stable Yard, St James's, SW1 (*early Victorian town mansion*)
London Museum, Kensington Palace, W8 (*major collection illustrating the history of London*)
Royal Mews Department, Buckingham Palace Road, SW1
Science Museum, Exhibition Road, South Kensington, SW7

Guide

DAVID PIPER   *Companion Guide to London*   Fontana